A Treasury of Garden Verse

FOR FELICITY AND ROSALIND

A
TREASURY
OF
GARDEN
VERSE

Introduced by Margaret Elphinstone

CANONGATE

First published in 1990 by
Canongate Publishing Limited, Edinburgh

Introduction © Margaret Elphinstone 1990

British Library Cataloguing in Publication Data
A Treasury of garden verse.
  1. Poetry in English. Special Subjects: Gardens –
Anthologies
I. Elphinstone, Margaret
821.008036

ISBN 0-86241-298-6

Set in Trump and Galliard by
Rowland Phototypesetting Limited
Bury St Edmunds, Suffolk

Printed and bound in Great Britain by
Butler and Tanner Limited
Frome, Somerset

Contents

Acknowledgements

FOR PERMISSION to reprint the poems in this anthology, acknowledgement is made to the following:
for THE MALICE-DANCE by John Cowper Powys, from *Samphire*, published by Village Press, to the Estate of John Cowper Powys; for TWO GARDENS by Walter de la Mare, from *Collected Poems*, Faber and Faber, to the Literary Trustees of Walter de la Mare and the Society of Authors as their representative; for RESPONSE by Mary Ursula Bethell, from *Collected Poems 1950*, to the Estate of Mary Ursula Bethell; for PUTTING IN THE SEED by Robert Frost, from *The Poetry of Robert Frost*, ed. Edward Connery Lathem, to Jonathan Cape Ltd; for lines from THE SLEEPING BEAUTY, by Edith Sitwell, from *Collected Poems*, published by Macmillan, to David Higham Associates Ltd; for ONE FOOT IN EDEN by Edwin Muir, from *The Collected Poems of Edwin Muir*, reprinted by permission of Faber and Faber; for LA FIGLIA CHE PIANGE by T. S. Eliot, from *Collected Poems 1909–1962*, reprinted by permission of Faber and Faber; for lines from THE DEFEAT OF YOUTH, by Aldous Huxley, from *Collected Poems*, to Mrs. Laura Huxley, and to the Hogarth Press; for THE GARDENER by Robert Graves, from *Collected Poems 1975*, published by Cassell to A. P. Watt Ltd, on behalf of the Executors of the Estate of Robert Graves; for OH GRATEFUL COLOURS, BRIGHT LOOKS by Stevie Smith, from *The Collected Poems of Stevie Smith* (Penguin Modern Classics), to James Macgibbon; for JEREMIAH, THE TABBY CAT, STALKS IN THE SUNLIT GARDEN by A. L. Rowse, from *Collected Poems 1981*, published by Blackwood, Edinburgh; for SNOWFALL ON A COLLEGE GARDEN by Cecil Day Lewis, from *Collected Poems of C. Day Lewis*, ed. Ian Parsons, to the Executors of the Estate of C. Day Lewis and to Jonathan Cape Ltd; for THE SUNLIGHT ON THE GARDEN by Louis MacNeice, from *The Collected Poems of Louis MacNeice*, reprinted by permission of Faber and Faber; for THEIR LONELY BETTERS by W. H. Auden, from *Collected Poems* by W. H. Auden, reprinted by permission of Faber and Faber; for IN PRINCES STREET GAIRDENS by Robert Garioch, from *Complete Poetical Works*, ed. R. Fulton, to Ian Sutherland, and to Macdonald

Publishers, Edinburgh; *for* SCYTHING by Basil Dowling, from *Collected Works*, to The Caxton Press, Christchurch, New Zealand; *for* THE COLD GREEN ELEMENT by Irving Layton, used by permission of the Canadian Publishers, McClelland and Stewart, Toronto; *for* IN THE GARDEN VILLA CLEOBOLUS, by Lawrence Durrell, from *Collected Poems* by Lawrence Durrell, reprinted by permission of Faber and Faber; *for* THE GARDEN by R. S. Thomas, to Grafton Books; *for* WALKING IN GARDENS by Dylan Thomas, from *The Poems*, published by Dent, to David Higham Associates Ltd; *for* WINTER GARDEN by David Gascoyne, from *Collected Poems 1988*, reprinted by permission of Oxford University Press; *for* KENSINGTON GARDENS, part II of the poem 'A Tour of London' by Muriel Spark, from *Going up to Sothebys and other poems*, published by Macmillan, to David Higham Associates Ltd; *for* UNFRIENDLY FLOWERS by Martin Bell, from *Complete Poems*, ed. Peter Porter, reprinted by permission of Bloodaxe Books Ltd.; *for* WAR by Nigel Weir, reprinted by permission of Faber and Faber; *for* THE GARDEN by Keith Douglas, from *The Complete Poems of Keith Douglas*, ed. Desmond Graham (1978), reprinted by permission of Oxford University Press; *for* DAYDREAM IN A SANCTUARY AT YOUNG ISLAND, ST. VINCENT by A. L. Hendriks, from *Madonna of the Unknown Nation*, to A. L. Hendriks and Workshop Press; *for* JARDIN DES COLOMBIERES by Lauris Edmond, from *Selected Poems*, to Oxford University Press, Auckland, New Zealand; *for* GARDEN, WILDERNESS by Michael Hamburger, from *Michael Hamburger: Collected Poems*, to Michael Hamburger and to Carcenet Press; *for* MANTEGNA'S AGONY IN THE GARDEN by Elizabeth Jennings, from *Collected Poems* published by Carcenet, to David Higham Associates Ltd; *for* THE GARDEN OF THE GODS by Thom Gunn, from *Moly* by Thom Gunn, reprinted by permission of Faber and Faber Ltd; *for* HER GARDEN by Freda Downie, from *A Stranger Here*, reprinted by permission of Martin Secker and Warburg Limited; *for* THE MANOR GARDEN by Sylvia Plath, from *Collected Poems* by Sylvia Plath, published by Faber and Faber London, copyright Ted Hughes 1967 and 1981, by permission of Olwen Hughes; *for* DRAWINGS by Fleur Adcock, from *The Incident Book* by Fleur Adcock (1986), reprinted by permission of Oxford University Press; *for* CORNERS OF A CIRCLE by Tanar Baybars, from *Narcissus in a Dry Pool*, by Sidgwick and Jackson, publishers; *for* THE INFLUENCE COMING INTO PLAY: THE SEVEN OF PENTACLES by Marge Piercy, from *Circles in the Water: Selected Poems of Marge Piercy*. Copyright 1972, 1982 by Middlemarsh Inc.; *for* THE CHINA PEAR TREES by Les Murray, from *The Daylight Moon*, Carcenet 1988, to Les Murray; *for* GARDENER by Dom Moraes, to Penguin Books India Ltd, New Delhi; *for* MR. MCGREGOR'S GARDEN by Medbh McGuckian, to Medbh McGuckian.

Introduction

Introduction

GARDEN POETRY is about two levels of art, the garden and the poem, at the point where they connect. Both arise out of a particular culture and time, so that both display the same concepts in different artistic forms. The raw material of the poet is language; that of the gardener, nature. Garden poetry, when studied as a separate entity, becomes a point of double contact between the natural world and the world of ideas, an interface between two levels of creativity, which provides scope for a multitude of images.

A garden poem is not just an account of a garden or of gardening. There have been some excellent garden treatises written in verse, and no one would dare to deny that Virgil's *Georgics* are poetry, yet they also constitute a practical gardening book of which *The Reader's Digest* might be proud. Until the eighteenth century a gardening book was as likely to be in verse as in prose. Some of these verse treatises, for example those by Thomas Tusser and George Gascoigne, are still highly readable. Such works do not figure in this anthology, simply because if they were allowed a little space they would soon take over the whole.

There are many more poems about gardens than about gardening, and even more poems about nature untouched than there are about gardens. An anthologist has to be strict here: if nature has her way, and is allowed to grow rampant, the garden will be overrun. If the poems have no specific connection with the garden, they must be kept outside the gates. A garden can be many things, and within the long spectrum of English poetry it has been almost all of them. Some poets have been deeply concerned with the garden as an image of humanity's relationship to nature. They focus on what is being done with, or to, nature, and why. It is sensitive matter for a poet, who is personally concerned with imposing form upon diffused experience, and encapsulating and heightening life within the confines of an art. Occasionally poets have focussed specifically upon the parallels between the art of poetry and the art of creating gardens.

The garden as an image of love has stood the test of centuries.

Sometimes the garden is love itself, sometimes it is the background for the lovers; sometimes the lover's mistress is described in the image of the garden. 'Come into the garden Maud' is an invitation extended by many a poet to their lover since the fourteenth century.

The garden has remained a fruitful image for many of life's experiences. Turning from one poem to another, we see it as a symbol of renewal, retreat, artistic inspiration, or death. But poems are not mere symbols, and the garden is seldom a figure to which we can attach a neat label.

The poems here are arranged in chronological order so that the development of the garden both as physical entity and poetic image can be traced through history and so enlighten us concerning the complex layers of tradition and symbolism that we inherit today.

Obviously, the closer to our own time, the more accessible the language of a poem is likely to be. Middle English garden poetry is too good to miss entirely, so, where necessary, glosses have been provided in the text. Some fifteenth, sixteenth and seventeenth century spellings have been modernised to make a poem more accessible. Where the original is unlikely to present difficulties to a general reader, it has been left unaltered. I have tried to treat each poem in the most appropriate manner, aiming at ease of reading rather than strict conformity.

THE GARDEN itself is a product of prosperous civilisation, developing alongside the other arts. The peasantry under the feudal system had no leisure for planting gardens. In 'The Nun's Priest's Tale', Chaucer describes what a poor family might do with a little land, if they had any. Chanticleer's mistress and her daughter owned cows, pigs and a sheep called Molly, as well as poultry. They grew a few vegetables in a 'bed of wortes', and some herbs. Peas and beans were field crops, but cabbages, leeks and onions were regarded as a sorry substitute or flavouring for meat. Vegetables were for fasts, not poetry.

In Chaucer's true garden poetry, we are in a world far removed from Chanticleer's yard. The poems and the gardens are closely related, both arising from the tradition of courtly love. The 'Romaunt of the Rose', like its French forebears, is a poem of courtly love centred upon a garden which is an image of love itself. The same can be said of James I's garden in 'The Kingis Quair'. Chaucer's garden may be entirely symbolic; James' garden is supposedly the real garden that he saw from his prison window. The difference is immaterial. There were such gardens, planted and laid out as carefully as the words and images of a poem.

However, symbolism cannot account for everything. There were strong practical reasons why the gardens of the aristocracy developed as they did. In a country where civil war was rife, there was no place for spacious gardens. Nor was it possible to give priority indoors to comfort, light, air, beauty or privacy. Small walled castle gardens, developed out of the need for defence, also fitted the current poetic image.

Langland's garden, which God himself made 'Amyddes man's body', belongs to another world of symbolism, this time that of Medieval Christian tradition. The garden in 'Piers the Ploughman' is a parable of a kind familiar from the Miracle Plays, and familiar too in the design of monastery and nunnery gardens. Langland describes a garden of which the centre is the tree of charity, whose roots are pity and mercy, and whose branches are good deeds, where the ground is hoed and cultivated by the good work of Piers, a gardener in the employment of Christ. The image is poetic, but one that might impinge all the more powerfully upon those who heard it, because it was real and familiar.

A wealth of lyrics from the fifteenth and sixteenth centuries express courtly love or Christian belief in the imagery of garden plants, and often within the garden itself. Lilies and roses abound, but other garden flowers are frequently mentioned by name. The ubiquitous gillyflower has been variously identified as wallflower, pinks or stocks. It originally meant any sweet-smelling flower, deriving its name from the French for a clove tree.

The poet of 'The Gardener' is unusually botanical. He gives us several flowers by name: the primrose, the gillyflower, sweet william, camovine, marigold and blaewort (cornflower). In these he figuratively dresses his lady, offering each flower as a garment, but then she turns the image on its head, so that the flowers become intimations of mortality, replacing the beauty of summer with the sombre garments of winter, east wind, rain or snow.

We begin to see that very often the garden image is double-edged. The garden reflects nature; often it represents love in terms of nature. In the fourteenth and fifteenth centuries the world may have been more beautiful, but it was perhaps more consistently cruel. Many garden lyrics focus on the extraordinary joy of spring and summer with an intensity that may seem strange to us, then introduce death in the form of winter snow or March wind, with an abrupt twist of the garden image. Love and youth, like the flowers in the garden, are transient, and a sense of mortality is never far below the surface. A lighthearted lyric like 'I have a newe garden' focuses on sexuality and regeneration; a more sombre poem like 'The Gardener' turns from images of life towards death. These lyrics were the popular songs of their day, and those that we have are certainly only a fraction of those that are lost. In a society where neither birth nor death could be disguised, and where one could quickly turn to the other, the pattern of the seasons in the garden was a poignant reflection of human experience.

Often the gardens in Renaissance poetry remain Medieval in conception, and in fact British gardens often remained closed and compact long after the fashion (and conditions) for wide spaces and broad walks was established elsewhere. The old symbolism of the flowers also prevails. In Joshua Sylvester's 'The Garden', the flowers become the pleasures of life: violets, marigolds, gillyflowers (here used as a synonym for pinks), and pansies. Death, like winter, kills joy 'with sudden cold'. This is not ostensibly a love poem, although it uses images of the traditional love lyric. Sylvester's bed of flowers might have been cultivated by Piers the Ploughman, as an illustration of the dominion of Death over Worldly Pleasure.

Like his language, Spenser's 'Garden of Adonis' in *The Faerie Queene*, seems deliberately archaic. The garden is girt in by high walls, with an entrance of double gates. Like the enclosed garden of the 'Romaunt of the Rose' the gates are guarded by a porter. The enemy within the garden is the age-old foe of summer beauty, Time, who with his scythe 'Does mow the flowring herbes and goodly things'. The Garden of Adonis represents the world into which souls pass. They are equipped with mortal bodies by the Porter Genius as they pass through the gate. The archaic tone of the poem might lead us to suppose that we are back in the world of Medieval Christian symbolism. However, the following lines suggest something quite different. The souls return through the gate when their life in the garden is over, but no final judgment follows. They return 'clad with other hew', still part of the cycle, 'So like a wheel around they runne from old to new.'

Perhaps it is fanciful to draw a parallel between the formal knot garden, neatly containing the abundance of nature, and the sonnet, whose economy of form could hold within it so great a wealth of language. Certainly there is a similar satisfaction to be found in both; the stringent containment gives an intensity to the living content which heightens its effect upon us. There are few knot gardens to be seen now, but those that there are give an impression of vitality within order. A vibrancy comes across in sixteenth century garden poetry which may have been a matter of fact as well as language. The truth is that garden flower varieties were not as bright as they are today, and yet Constable's 'violet of purple colour . . . dyed with the blood she made my heart to shed', Campion's 'rosebuds fill'd with snow', or Shakespeare's 'deep vermilion of the rose' leave us with a vivid impression of colour. By our standards they were writing about gardens that were not particularly colourful, but where form was paramount. The inference is that form heightens vision. Since plant breeding has become more important, the emphasis in the garden since the seventeenth century has been on changing the plants. They have become bigger and brighter than anything Shakespeare saw, but perhaps there has been a corresponding loss in perception.

Shakespeare, in his garden scenes, takes us into the heart of the sixteenth and seventeenth century garden, combining the details of practical gardening and the poetic image into a broad vision that is also immediate and familiar. Throughout the plays he repeatedly refers to aspects of gardening: manuring, weeding, setting seeds, pruning, grafting, the effects of sun and frost, flowers in season, pests, and so on. In some plays the imagery of the garden is a major and consistent theme.

Hamlet is filled with images of bad husbandry in relation to political neglect and abuse of power. The history plays are permeated with the same image: England as a garden or orchard, suffering from neglect, lack of weeding, careless pruning, rampant pests and untreated plant diseases.

This is new. Shakespeare clearly knows about gardening, and in his hands the poetic image is able to expand to absorb the reality of gardening, and so develop into something larger. The scene in the Duke of York's garden (from *Richard II*) expresses political meaning in the precise realities of pruning. Anyone who has pruned a fruit tree has snipped the ends off 'too-fast growing sprays', and learns to judge when they have become 'too lofty'. A gardener will also recognise the moment of pushing back broad spreading leaves to find a host of lanky weeds sheltering underneath. The considered removal of superfluous branches, that bearing boughs may live, appeals to the gardener's exercise of skill. The concept begins to emerge: it is necessary to have a skilled eye to judge correctly and act appropriately. Due weight is given at the beginning; the pruner must be 'like an executioner'. Because the gardening metaphors so accurately reflect actual gardening, we fully recognise the qualities of good government, though we may not ourselves be kings.

Act IV Scene II of *The Winter's Tale* probably contains the most famous discussion on grafting there is. Yet it could have taken place over the hedge of a Warwickshire cottage garden, perhaps not in blank verse, but with precisely the same subject matter. The poetic meaning is allowed to emerge without disturbing the realism. The garden, as Tusser would have assumed, belongs to Perdita as the woman of the house. If she objects to grafting, that is her decision. Her audience, like Polixenes, might have found her too nice, since improved carnations and gillyflowers were now standard cottage garden stock. However, she does keep the necessary stock of herbs for the kitchen. To her first audience, Perdita must have been an entirely recognisable figure, and yet she also belongs in the poetic world. There is a double irony in her speech with Polixenes. Not only do they both tell us more than they know, since we hold all the secrets of their identity, but also, Perdita herself is not the unadulterated child of nature. In the world of the play she is the lost daughter of Hermione and Leontes; in the marriage of rural life and poetic artifice she may have one foot in Warwickshire, but the other is in Arcadia. She does not yet know herself.

Richard Barnfield's 'Daphnis to Ganymede', in spite of its classic pastoral title, could also be seen as a celebration of the emerging cottage garden. It certainly belongs in Arcadia: the invitation to 'come and dwell with me' in rural bliss reminds us of Marlowe's passionate shepherd, but the pleasures offered here are more specific. 'Dwell with me *at home*' offers Daphnis, and goes on to describe what he has to offer in substantial detail. The garden plot contains the standard 'flowers to smell, roots to eat, and herbs for the pot'. There is even an arbour, surrounded by beds of lilies and roses. The flowers and herbs are listed by their country names. In addition, there are rabbits, goats, pigeons and a lamb. Ganymede is clearly not about to live a life of idleness.

In 1611, the Authorised Version of the English Bible was published. Access to its contents in the vernacular was no longer new, but the prose poetry that we now think of as Biblical has never been surpassed. Of course the image of the Garden of Eden has haunted European literature for as long as it has existed. In setting this translation among the other garden poems, one has a curious sense that this is the touchstone. It is the one image that every poet who has written in English about a garden must have had lurking in his or her consciousness. Many have referred to it specifically, many more have suggested the connection, subliminally or consciously. It is common knowledge or, less prosaically, myth. Because the reader will recognise it, it is readily available for new meanings and contexts. Perhaps it is salutary to give renewed attention to the version that has now become definitive. The first surprise is that it is so short. Like a Blake watercolour, where the image is so powerful that one expects a huge canvas, one expects a Miltonian epic. Instead, we have a terse account, barely covering one chapter. The extract here takes us to the Biblical origin of the woman/garden image that remains dominant, at least for so long as most of the poets who are available to us are male. We seem to have come a long way from the Garden of Love, and yet the characters bear some relation. There is the man, the protagonist, with whose story, or moral development, the action concerns itself. In the garden he encounters something Other, in this case evil rather than love, to whom he is brought by a woman. Here, she is the cause of his guilt and shame. We still live with the myth. Poets have used the garden image in a multitude of ways, but there is no escaping the parallel with Eden.

The seventeenth century poets developed the image, sometimes with a highly idiosyncratic relation, between image and idea. Garden poetry was very often still love poetry, but with a new flexibility. Eden is present in the background, but it too is no longer fixed. The old imagery, and the new treatment of it, often created an ironic contrast. There is a sense of tension as the old motifs are stretched to fit new ways of seeing a situation.

Donne's 'Twick'nam Garden', for instance, plays with the image of Eden, using it to express a highly individual point of view. He dazzles us with unexpected images, that force the old garden symbolism into new juxtapositions, that surprise us into a new outlook. The garden is equated with Paradise, but not by description. To prove it, the poet tells us, he has brought the serpent into it with him. A moment earlier, his metaphor was 'the spider love', whose powers seem to be closer to those of a sawfly or flea beetle, since it converts the manna of the garden to gall, but that by the way.

So the serpent in this Eden is Love, and we are told that the perils of winter would be more wholesome in the garden. Again, convention is flouted; the danger of death is subordinated to the falseness of women, the 'perverse sex', who are true to themselves in being false, and therefore destroy the lover by truth. The final couplet, in its juggling with truth, serves as the final ironic diminishment of all that has been felt.

Shirley's 'The Garden' again turns preconceptions upside down. He connects the old images to ideas almost contrary to convention; exploding each pre-conception is a series of small shocks which startle the reader into making a new connection every time. The first verse suggests something of Perdita's scorn of 'art of men', which purchases nature at a price, which – and this is the first shock – 'would stock old Paradise again'. What kind of Paradise is achieved by putting a price on Nature? We associate Eden with Nature, the innocent, unfallen state, but here, Paradise is gained by bargaining Nature away. The myth is turned on its head, and a question about gardening becomes a question about a whole value system.

Shirley goes on to reject one well-worn image after another. He wants a garden 'Where might I with the sun agree'. Naturally, we think, until we find that the agreement is that the sun will keep out of his garden. He rejects the new tulips, which were at the time of writing the very height of garden fashion, and turns back to the old flowers, violets, lilies and roses. But then we hear that the lilies and roses are not to open, unless for 'The sighs of lovers'. No joys of love here.

The central theme finally emerges as being the perfidy of women. One is reminded of Donne's 'Go and catch a falling star', where the conclusion seems almost banal after the thrilling images of the opening lines. However, a closer look at Shirley's conclusion shows no diminishment. The lover wants to exclude accepted beauty from his garden, making it both a tomb and a fortress against women, but we are not meant to sympathise completely:

> No bird shall live within my pale
> To charm me with their shames of art.

Tulips might be suspected as artifice, but songbirds? We cannot be supposed to agree that this is artful seduction, and so we are brought to view the epitaph of the last lines with ironic detachment.

In George Herbert's 'The Flower' we find the same play on the image of Paradise turned to a completely different purpose. The poem begins with the age-old delight in spring and renewal, here equated with the gifts of God. But then the next verse is almost a reversal; the poet rejoices at the regeneration in his heart, then sinks back to the dormancy of winter. Paradise becomes the place beyond death and regeneration – 'O that I once past changing were!' But then the final verses go further, into an appreciation, not of eternal rest, but of both summer and winter. The verse 'And now in age I bud again' is a moving testament to the joy that comes only after adversity. The wonders of God are the whole of life, not just the summer of it. God's garden has expanded in concept since the Paradise of verse three, to embrace experience, so that those who have survived the tempest are the ones who can put aside their pride, and enter.

Beaumont's 'The Garden' is another religious poem which takes the Eden image as a developing theme in a swift argument that concludes that the real paradise is 'on open Calvarie'. In contrast to the garden centred upon the tree of crucifixion, the original Eden is seen as a merciless image of unattainable innocence which only torments the fallen who are forever shut out. The poet is excluded by 'a flaming sword' to be left at the mercy of the serpent sin, which Eden has also failed to harbour. The unexpectedness of the imagery demands our attention; we are brought to a devotional conclusion almost without realising it, by a series of riddles.

The most famous seventeenth century Eden is undoubtedly Milton's, in 'Paradise Lost'. His garden, in Restoration times, differs from that of the earlier poets, in that it is a whole countryside, not a cultivated garden within walls entered by a gate. God's garden is the whole earth, not a formally cultivated area shut away from it. Perhaps this change is hardly surprising, when the wider landscape was beginning to alter perceptibly under the onslaught of civilisation. Until now the garden had been an oasis of order amidst the chaos of wilderness, but the balance was changing. The wilderness was no longer the outer world, the place of banishment from the garden. From now on, it is possible to see the original Garden *as* the wilderness, the unsullied piece of nature safely contained, apart from the human world without.

Thus Milton's Paradise is on the grand scale. It is the natural world before the Fall, a countryside uncontaminated by the presence of fallen man. The account of Eden in Book IV is a description of idealised nature, without the element of art that we associate with gardens.

Nor is Milton's Paradise an exclusively Biblical garden. The extract here gives dominion over the spring to Pan, and goes on to compare Eden favourably with 'that field of Enna' where Dis abducted Proserpine. Milton's garden imagery is drawn from the Old Testament, classical legend, Medieval romance, recent discoveries of an apparently untainted paradise across the Atlantic, and contemporary garden convention. The passage here, which is the description of Eden itself, the very heart of the Paradise image in the poem, depicts the garden almost entirely in terms of classical allusion. And yet his theme does not deviate from the Old Testament story; the classical parallels serve to underline the religious basis of the poem. Proserpine was snatched from the fair field of Enna; Daphne was torn from her sweet grove; Bacchus was not left to enjoy his Nyseian Isle. The innocence of the garden is transient and beset by dangers. Each of the Greek legends ends in rape or violence. The garden cannot be trusted; we have to look beyond it to something which is more enduring. On that note the Fiend is introduced, who sees 'undelighted all delight'. The other gardens, with their implications of future violence, have already aroused foreboding, which intensifies when we see the Fiend looking down on the new creation in the garden including the two human beings who dwell within it.

The struggle between human artifice and nature was one that deeply concerned Andrew Marvell, who returned to the garden theme in several poems. 'The Mower Against Gardens' is his most impassioned protest against artificiality in gardens, imposed by humanity upon imprisoned nature. He refers briefly to the lifelessness of the formal garden, where luxurious man:

> First enclosed within the Garden's square
> A dead and standing pool of air.

However, the main theme of the poem is artificiality in the form of grafting. Neither traditional nor new plants were exempt, and, unlike most poets, Marvell even casts an eye on what was occurring in the kitchen garden, where many old vegetable varieties had been improved. He also deprecates the contemporary search of 'other worlds, through oceans new' for new plant material. In contrast to this forced artifice, he turns to the 'wild and fragrant innocence' of nature. It is, however, the nature of Arcadian pastoral, presided over by fauns and satyrs.

If Marvell saw grafting as an exercise in seduction, one wonders what he would have made of the discovery, fifteen years after his death, that plants are sexually differentiated, and that deliberate cross-breeding was possible. In Marvell's time a pink or striped tulip was still a matter for remark, as witness Robert Herrick, who probably wrote more poems about tulips than any other poet. The ancient skill of grafting was coming under new scrutiny, as its effects were combined with the influx of so many non-native plants.

If I had to choose one poem that captures the essence of the garden, it would almost certainly be Marvell's 'The Garden'. Here, the poet has come to terms with the garden itself, and is at peace within it. Although the Eden image is used, the garden is neither unattainable nor somewhere else. The poem is in the present tense, and the language is that of immediate experience – the words 'here' and 'this' are reiterated throughout. Marvell is in a real garden, it seems, looking, touching, eating the fruits, listening, lying on the moss. Through present experience he attains spiritual freedom:

> Casting the Bodies Vest aside
> My soul into the Boughs doth glide.

The garden is the point of knowing, the place to be. It may, and does, lead him to speculation, to consideration of other gardens, classical and Biblical, and into a contemplation of deeper meaning; but the meaning is also contained within the garden. Being in the garden becomes the experience of living.

In the eighteenth century, formality in the garden was still generally regarded as human order created out of wilderness, and for the great landscapers this remained the dominant theme for another century. But in some gardens the reaction to lost Eden was already under way. The most famous of these was Alexander Pope's, at Twickenham. It stretched down to the banks of the Thames, a tunnel being built under the road for access. Pope turned this tunnel into a grotto, adorning it with rocks, shells, glass to reflect the lamplight, and a spring. The walls were studded with fossils, unusual stones, or statuary. The grotto survives, although the rest of the garden has gone. This was in fact extensive, comprising a lawn enclosed by trees, a vista of a distant obelisk, shrubberies with walks, a kitchen garden, and a vineyard.

The whole thing sounds about as wild as an iambic pentameter, but then, nature was still abundant enough to make strict conservation an unnecessary concept. For Addison and Pope, parterres and clipped hedges constituted excess of art, and artificial grottoes, cascades, lawns and groves constituted nature. One of Pope's satires lists an absurd catalogue of items of topiary for sale, in mockery of the formal garden. In more serious poetry, he insists that due account be taken of what nature has provided: 'consult the genius of the place in all.'

Pope's garden of Alcinous presents 'beauteous order' within its 'allotted space', and, carefully separated from the world, the garden within is given over to total abundance. Pope's idea of a return to nature may seem in the light of hindsight to be hedged about by the traditions and conventions of contemporary thought. This does not invalidate it. Both his garden and his garden poetry represented a new influx of energy which had decayed as old forms grew sterile. Moreover, the re-connection with nature was quite genuine. Pope's garden was a place of contemplation. The grotto was a place apart, enclosed, and yet connected. Secluded within it, one could see the boats passing on the Thames, the movement of water and of human life. It represents the relationship between landscape and human perception, and so, figuratively speaking, it becomes the place in which poetry can be written. The poet, enclosed within the garden and yet connected to the world, can find a voice.

John Gay's 'The Butterfly and the Snail', taken from his fables, conveys nothing so subtle. Here, nature has become subordinated to a fairly simple moral. The interest is the Aesop-like conclusion, 'Snail was I born, and snail shall end.' There is a certain doggedness to it, like digging the garden on a wet day.

Turning from Pope to Thomson, we move from one concept of nature to another. Thomson's 'Seasons' belong in a highly ordered landscape, which, like his poetry, appear far more English than Scottish. Even when he refers to the mountains, there is a smoothness of tone and language that conjures up the contours of southern England rather than his native Borders. Furthermore, the poem lacks immediacy; it is literary description rather than individual experience. One feels that Thomson is not writing from a figurative grotto, but from a point of vantage, from which he can survey a landscape spread out below. 'Spring Flowers' seems closer to a nurseryman's catalogue than an impassioned response. Nor can flower breeding be regarded with anything but comfortable satisfaction. The 'exulting florist', regarding the varied colours of the tulip, 'marks with secret pride, the wonders of his hand'. This is nature tamed and organised, kept firmly in order by the hand of man.

William Mason's 'The English Garden' is also very much a garden in prospect. Mason was strongly influenced by Thomas Gray, whose aesthetic approach was to define the perfect view, with the aid of 'Claude glasses', and then to contemplate it as a set piece. Mason likewise deliberately surveys what he sees, often specifically in terms of the visual arts:

> so to spread
> A canvas, which, when touch'd by autumn's hand
> Shall gleam with dusky gold, or russet rays . . .

In contrast, Joseph Warton demonstrates the new longing for Gothic ruggedness and irregularity. He turns from the gardens at Versailles with disgust, equating the oppression of a people with the oppression and torture of nature. He turns instead to the wild landscape which was now becoming fashionable, complete with precipices, waterfalls, blasted heaths and mournful evergreens. But even in this Gothic Eden, we are invited to contemplate the Prospect, in which ripe harvests compete with Gothic ruins for our attention, and the moaning dove is pitied by a milkmaid who seems to derive directly from Arcadia.

Cowper's description of Capability Brown's work in 'The Task' expresses a similar view. He laments the passing of woods, hills and valleys, and the homes of our forefathers – 'a grave whisker'd race – But tasteless'. The satiric note warns us how to take the account that follows. Cowper moves from regret for nature's passing to the spectacle of bankruptcy facing those who have indulged in too much improvement. However, it took a Goldsmith to face the social implications squarely. His description of the village only hints at the former place of the cottage garden, but it is included here as a garden poem without apology. It places the new landscape of wealth disguised as Arcadia squarely in its social context. The Enclosure Acts which had allowed Brown's employers to create their landscaped parks had also had their impact on the gardens of other classes. Goldsmith takes us from a question of taste to a matter of social conscience.

The small poem by Robert Burns forms a different kind of contrast to the earlier essays in taste. 'The gard'ner wi' his paidle' seemed almost to have disappeared in the great debate between art and nature.

Few poets since Shakespeare seem to have considered how 'busy busy are his hours', which suggests that the poets were not themselves the gardeners. Burns' poem, typically, is deceptively simple. It is not naive, its deliberate use of Scots might be regarded as a considered alternative to English sentimentalism. Outside Arcadia, spring is a time for hard digging and sexuality, not seen through Claude's glasses and rhapsodised over, but experienced.

From this point on, the garden image takes on a new lease of life. No longer turned in on itself, it begins once again to reflect human emotions and experience. Blake's 'The Garden of Love' is manifestly a Song of Experience; The Garden of Love, as in the Songs of Innocence, represents the innocent state, in this case desecrated by the image of the chapel. It has become filled with tombstones, and typically 'Priests in black gowns were walking their rounds,' Blake's treadmill of institutionalised selfishness destroys spontaneous life. For Blake, real knowledge came through use of the Imagination. The garden in these poems becomes an aspect of Imagination itself. So far from being something outside, or far away, it has become the process of life itself. It is the antithesis of spectacle, or vista. Blake might be said to have re-integrated the garden image into poetic experience.

Perhaps the best description we have of the making of a real eighteenth century garden is in the diaries of Dorothy Wordsworth, in which she describes the creating and planting of the garden at Dove Cottage. She and William employed a gardener, but they also did much of the work themselves. William did most of the digging. They stocked their garden with plants from other cottagers and from the wild. They also took to establishing garden plants out on the fells, to the possible confusion, Dorothy notes, of later botanists. She also describes their leisure hours in the garden; they had an arbour, in which they read Shakespeare on summer afternoons.

Turning from Dorothy to William, it is hardly surprising to find an *embarras de richesse* of garden poetry. 'A Farewell' was chosen for its evocation of the poet's feelings for his own garden. He sees the garden within its context of mountains and valley, then turns to the details within it, the shrubs by the door, the daisies and marsh marigolds. He refers to his own part in its creation, how he brought plants from the fields around. There is no element of set description; the garden and his feeling for the garden are fused together in the language of intense personal experience. In leaving his garden for two months, the poet is leaving part of himself, which justifies the emotion of the farewell.

Much of Wordsworth's garden poetry is about gardening. It focuses on practical tasks, like pruning, or upon the gardener's relationship to his work, as in his attachment to a wellworn spade. Wordsworth also reveals a gardener's eye view of the garden. He notices hidden corners, particular flowers, plants tucked away behind rocks. He refers to the sowing of the seed, or the planting, when he looks at the grown flower. The sonnet 'In a Garden in the grounds of Coleorton, Leicestershire', contrasts the formal garden prospect to just such a vignette. The little niche will indeed survive the temples, columns and towers, because it will exist as part of the poet's experience, if nowhere else.

Coleridge reflects upon a similar garden to that at Dove Cottage, also surrounded by Lakeland hills. The poem's combination of introspection and detailed natural description are reminiscent of Wordsworth's garden poetry. However, the style seems more reminiscent of Cowper, and indeed the theme takes us from the little Cot, with its myrtles and jasmine and 'little landscape round', to a full prospect of mountains, fields, river, seats, lawns and Abbey, then on to cities, islands and shoreless ocean. The progression leads us from the poet's own garden, and his intimate relation to it, via an eighteenth century vista of all that can be surveyed, into an almost mystical world:

God methought
Had built him there a temple,

within which the whole outer world is reflected. The pattern is repeated; once again the poet's leavetaking takes us to an image of the cosmos, this time in terms of 'Science, freedom and the Truth in Christ'. The final return to the garden emerges as hope expressed in a universal prayer, 'Let thy kingdom come'. The cottage garden has become a catalyst for exploring universal truths in a meditative style, with a hint of the magical element of 'Kubla Khan' as one kind of reality merges into another.

Leigh Hunt's 'A House and Grounds' takes us back to the larger country house garden, but there have been perceptible changes even here. Although we are back with Park and Prospect, the emphasis is on flowers again; indeed the house itself is 'half hid with blooms'. The grounds are to 'keep a look' of nature, with birds, a brook, an area for flowers, and the rest turf and trees, a definition of nature which by now seems familiar. There is no vegetable garden, but there is a walk, and a bowling green.

The second generation of Romantic poets moved even further from formal gardening tradition. Shelley's 'Osimandus' satirises formal taste, and the rules that defined the correct observation and appreciation of a set landscape. In his garden in 'The Sensitive Plant', he gives us something very different. The garden is not viewed objectively, but felt, as it is imbued with the power of the Lady 'Whose form was upborne by a lovely mind'. This garden is all air and no earth: so far from doing any weeding or pruning, the lady's very step pities the ground on which it treads. There is a paradox; this is a garden poem, yet, like the lady's footsteps, contact with the earth remains reluctant. Images of light, sprinkled water, insects that barely touch the plants, confirm the impression. Flowers have no names, but they do have feelings, and an awareness of the spirit that is transmitted by the lady's glowing fingers. There is no substance to this garden, and in the last line, the poet abruptly indicates that he knows it: 'And ere the first leaf looked brown – she died.'

Byron's garden is just as ethereal. Again, the theme is summer beauty that is destroyed by time. The roses of love, pruned by the unmerciful knife of Time, become the setting for Love's Last Adieu. The garden image of the first verse has the effect of setting a scene in drama. The backdrop is the garden, which adds substance by reflecting the soliloquy on love against an external image. It also gives a framework to the fleeting garden images, making the poem visual in effect as well as emotional.

The garden image still stands in these poems. It is coherent and integrated, but the garden has become idealised out of reality. It seems to exist only as part of the poet's inner world. The pursuit of nature has finally taken us out of the external world altogether, and into a dreamlike inner vision. Curiously enough, the poem by Peacock, taken from the satiric *Misfortunes of Elphin*, a work in an entirely different style, has a similar effect. The apple orchard does not reflect intense personal feeling, but it is nevertheless idealised rather than actual, a dream garden created out of sixth century legend and Medieval romance. Peacock had already satirised modern landscaping fashions in *Headlong Hall*; it is interesting that his own garden vision apparently belongs to a dream world.

However, the real cottage garden remains a consistent theme throughout the nineteenth century. John Clare wrote many poems about the actual gardens of Northamptonshire. Unlike the Wordsworths, he was born a countryman, and his poems about cottage life, gardens, and the country surrounding them are written from inside experience of village life. His love for his own country and tradition is quite removed from romantic appreciation. He observes with a matter-of-fact intensity which infuses an apparently simple poem with vibrant energy. The 'Proposals for Building a Cottage' describes a cottage garden, with its fence around it, woodbine trained to the wall, a seat of turf by the door, surrounded by roses and other sweet-smelling flowers. The poem moves from dynamic descriptions of the birds, sparrows pulling at the thatch, swallows sweeping in flight, to the slower tempo of activity indoors. The nearest we come to explicit emotion is

> And then I'll thank ye for the gift
> As something worth the giving.

The understatement of the countryman becomes an ironic climax, making us realise how much feeling has gone into the apparently bald description that preceded it.

Both Thomas Hood's 'I remember' and William Barnes' 'The Hwomestead' celebrate similar gardens in their different ways. Whereas Barnes' poem remains static in theme, sustaining one note of rustic contentment, Hood's poem is retrospective. The garden, by virtue of belonging to a lost childhood, has become one of the inaccessible gardens of the imagination.

The gardens of poetic imagination and the actual gardens of Victorian Britain were now parting company so radically that it is tempting to see the difference as a major dislocation between inner and outer worlds. Tennyson did not invite Maud to come and admire the carpet bedding. Even when the gardens in Victorian poems are real, they are intensely private and individual. The diversity of styles and fashions in the garden left room for some people to create something of their own in their gardens. The garden at Haworth, for example, was about as far removed from the new parks and gardens as one could possibly get. Perhaps the true keynote of the Victorian garden is individuality in spite of prevailing convention. This may provide a clue to the poems.

The garden in 'Maud' is a garden of heavy scents. Spice and musk are introduced in the first stanza, coupled with the oppressive image of 'The black bat, night', so suggesting the kind of hot, still night when garden scents grow richer, almost cloying the senses. In the third stanza sounds are added to scents, until the past night seems overheated and hectic, while still sweet and enticing. In this context the rose becomes identified with the night's feverish passion, which infuses the whole of 'Maud'. The other flowers become caught up in the drama of love, so that the whole garden reflects the almost frenzied passion of the lovers. The garden is swept by the oppressive energy that promises storms. The speed of the rhythm, and the disjointed exclamations of the red rose, the white rose and the lily suggest the rapid pulse and palpitating heart of intense, perhaps unhealthy, passion.

We are back with the garden as the image of love, but could not be further from the serenity of a summer's day. The woman/garden simile is no longer the conventional image of love; instead we have a more personal, perhaps more tortured metaphor, in which private emotion has infused the garden, so that it seems to exist solely as a mirror of the emotions. The Renaissance garden encompassed two worlds within the poem, the real garden and the symbol of the emotions. Tennyson's garden seems to be absorbed entirely into the world of the emotions.

Browning's poem from 'Garden Fancies' is both more colloquial in tone and more sharply realised, in terms of the picture of a woman within a real garden. The emotional response is implicit in the way the narrative is presented. The first line shows clearly that the narrator is a lover, but his feelings emerge through his description of his love moving about the garden. In fact, all that we learn about her is that she is sensitive to the garden, pointing out details, and giving names to the flowers. It is through the garden itself that we regard her. The garden is so sharply defined, even down to the squeaking wicket gate, that, as the image develops, playing upon the comparison between the Spanish lady and the rose, we seem to gain a specific impression of her.

Elizabeth Barret Browning's garden uses the image of the garden brought into her 'close room' in the shape of flowers given to her by her lover, and develops it to equate herself with the garden 'overgrown with bitter weeds and rue', waiting for her lover's weeding. But, like a garden, she also has flowers to give, and in the final couplet she instructs her lover to keep regarding her flowers in their true colours, and to remember that their roots still grow in her. It is interesting that in this garden poem by a woman, she takes the old woman/garden image, and makes it subjective, using it to express her own point of view. Anne Bronte's 'The Arbour' uses the familiar motif of winter's chill signifying death, but in her poem the vision of summer turns out to be illusory in the first place. The clear sky was made blue by frost, the green and glossy leaves are winter evergreens, the rustling in the branches is the chill of winter. The poem ends with no expectation of change or summer, while the spirit is held down by chains of death. Once again we see a well-worn image turned to express an individual point of view.

Arnold's 'Lines written in Kensington Gardens' is one of the first poems we have that is set in a city park. Once the country became relatively inaccessible to many city-dwellers, we begin to find poems about nature sequestered and enclosed within green places within the town. It is made the more precious in contrast to the urban wilderness without. The enclosed Medieval garden was an oasis shut away from natural wilderness without and the pressures of human life indoors. Here, the garden is reinstated as a place of retreat, this time from urban wilderness. It is interesting to contrast this poem with the garden description in 'The Scholar Gipsy', in which the garden is an integral part of the pastoral scene, the centre point of an Arcadian world. 'The Scholar Gipsy' is ostensibly set in a pre-industrial world; in Kensington Gardens 'The rural Pan' exists within the context of 'the huge world, which roars hard by'. Typically Arnold relates the quest for rural peace to the lifelong search for inner peace, which is invoked in the last verse as a hope rather than a present experience. The garden is merely a signpost towards deeper contentment, which is not apprehendable. Thus the poem presents us with a contemporary predicament set within a contemporary garden.

A noticeable feature of nineteenth century garden poetry is the difference between British and American garden poems. Whitman's 'This compost' has nothing to do with the literary garden images that have by now become so familiar. The poem is about the healing, regenerative power of the soil, the compost that can turn what is sick, decayed and sour into the material from which clean waters and new fruits can spring. It is a poem about earth, and the power of earth. As such, it is the antithesis of Shelley's garden of the air, although that too was radical in its time. In Whitman's poem the earth becomes divine:

Now I am terrified at the Earth, it is that calm and patient,
It grows such sweet things out of such corruption.

Arnold's 'Calm soul of all things' seems palely intellectual against this vivid comprehension of spirit within soil. Just as Whitman's rhythms and language were radical, so his concept of the earth is exciting and vigorous when set against older conventions.

Emily Dickinson wrote so many garden poems that to choose two is bound to seem an arbitrary process, especially as her garden poems in sequence build up an impressionistic picture of her whole relationship to her garden. 'All these my banners be' is perhaps as definitive of her work as it is possible for one poem to be, but the two chosen here are perhaps undeservedly less well known. Both relate the present experience in the garden to the 'riddle', the paradox of living and dying. One highly focused moment thus becomes a microcosm of universal experience.

The pre-Raphaelites produced very different garden poems. As the movement was rooted in the visual arts, with an eye to nature as it manifested itself in an idealised Medieval world, one would expect to find the garden presented as an other-world of beauty and meaning. Dante Gabriel Rossetti's 'The Trees of the Garden' considers human mortality against the longevity of the trees. He cites the earth itself, and the trees that are rooted in it, as having the answer to the problem of time and mortality, but his question remains curiously abstract. In comparison with Whitman's evocation of living soil, Rossetti's earth seems unrealised, reducing the question from lived experience to a philosophical proposition.

Kipling's 'The Glory of the Garden' is a song of praise for the kind of garden that was in fact beginning to disappear, but there is no note of irony in the refrain 'For the glory of the Garden it shall never pass away.' The poem is about the gardeners, and Kipling dwells upon aspects of the garden normally kept out of sight: the dungpits, cold frames and potting sheds, and upon the hard labour that goes into creating so much beauty. As in much of Kipling's writing, there is a note of half-truth that verges on sentiment. 'Our England is a Garden' is a statement that requires the overriding rhythm to sustain it; given a moment's pause, and the reader becomes too aware of the other side of the picture. As it stands, the poem reflects the nostalgic yet down to earth picture of the declining great gardens.

Yeats' 'Ancestral Houses' considers the same subject matter in utterly dissimilar fashion:

Some violent bitter man, some powerful man
Called architect and artist in, that they,
Bitter and violent men, might rear in stone
The sweetness that all longed for night and day . . .

The garden as a place apart, a tranquil retreat separate from the world, is invoked only to be dispelled as illusion. The beautiful garden is a monument to 'the inherited glory of the rich'. Perhaps in Ireland, in the throes of civil war, the irony that could be avoided in England was inescapable. For the garden is a work of art. In the second verse Yeats counterbalances the oppressive illusion of privilege with the upwelling joy in life that gives birth to inspiration. He has taken the garden of the imagination out of the illusory world of 'mere dream', and placed it within the bitter public world of violence and war. The paradox is that, exposed to the light of day, the dream garden remains valid. Greatness and bitterness are bound together, and there is no escaping either aspect of a two-edged inheritance.

George Sims' 'A Garden Song' is a facetious rendering of the old theme of the garden as a place apart, made ridiculous by the introduction of all the clichés of the modern suburban garden. The paradox was a real one; the 'sequestered close' of Austin Dobson's garden, or the red and white rose petals of O'Shaughnessy's 'Song' are like the dying echoes of an outworn song. On the other hand, Wilde's 'Magdalen Walks' successfully reiterates the old motif of delight in spring and the transience of joy, in a tone of immediate experience. The poem is in the present tense, the rhythm reflects the racing clouds and the quickened pulse of spring, and the conclusion twists the stereotype into something new. Love matters more than spring to humanity, and yet it exists only in the moment, while spring eternally recurs. Stevenson's 'To A Gardener' is equally robust. There is certainly the nostalgic vision of the cottage garden, but there is also relish for the actuality of rural life. The garden is full of useful vegetables, and the onion is given precedence over the rose, as the poet looks forward to a good meal rather than spiritual refreshment.

Alongside the nostalgic garden image, contemporary garden poems were being written that centred upon the meanings of gardens within the modern world. Thomas Hardy's 'Hampton Court' encapsulates the change. Hampton Court provides reminders of the past on the grand scale, but what the poet actually notices is the winter's day, the colour of trees and walls, and the sounds of birds. The enfeebled fountain is introduced as a background noise, which becomes insistent and ominous as the poem progresses. Hardy raises the ghosts of the past by an act of his own will, but they fade away, while 'the mindless fountain tinkling on' reduces the current of history from stereotyped pageant to present futility.

Old images are revoked, and in 'The Lodging House Fuchsias' a distinctive modern note is asserted. The flowers tell us about a woman, but the language seems almost casual, the rhythm echoes normal speech, and Mrs Masters is the landlady of a lodging house. The fuchsias lining the path are contemporary, but not prosaic. Robert Bridges' 'Cheddar Pinks' holds the two kinds of garden together in a deliberate tension, which, although somewhat self-conscious, draws the garden of escape into a modern world. It raises the authenticity of private indulgence in an older vision, as the poet reads Homer among his pinks, and its place in 'the busy world.'

Later, Edith Sitwell's poem sequence 'The Sleeping Beauty' took for its background a great house and garden. Within this context, the poem 'In the great gardens' focuses upon details of natural beauty that might be found in any garden: skies and stars, periwinkles, lilies-of-the-valley and forget-me-nots. A different note is struck through the similes, which refer to eighteenth century France, and then Weber waltzes, which makes the Princess a complex figure, caught between a wider, more sophisticated world, and the rustic world of the garden flowers. This gives a new twist to the old question in the last verse.

A new direction was given to twentieth century garden poetry, as the garden became an obvious motif for war poetry. E. W. Tennant's 'Home Thoughts in Laventie' is about a garden, still undesecrated by virtue of its separation from a ruined world. The poet connects the garden to the joy in life which still exists within him, and so turns to thoughts of home. Home, represented as a garden, suggests the inno-cence of unfallen Eden, through rural images of the past that conjure up a whole countryside still undespoiled. Yet the poem is one of action rather than meditation; sustained by a strong narrative, a swift rhythm and short, almost breathless lines, it suggests a brief moment of tranquility snatched from a world of horror. The 'we' in the garden have no time for idleness; they have to search and find. The words 'rest' and 'well content' allow only a momentary pause. After the destruction of the opening verses, the garden image has regained all the poignancy it ever had. A dream garden has become sanity, not self-indulgence, in a world that has turned to nightmare.

A generation later, Nigel Weir's 'War' took the war into the garden itself. Nothing is sacred or separate. The gardens themselves will be invaded and destroyed. Contemplating his own certain death 'fight-ing in the sky', and the desolation of the garden, the poet faces the destruction of all that matters to him with bitter insouciance. In the last line we discover that Eden is already ravaged; now that his friends are gone, there is nothing left in life but to go on killing until he too is dead. This is a terrifying end to the garden of the imagination.

And yet the Eden image prevailed throughout the twentieth cen-tury. Edwin Muir's 'One Foot in Eden' looks from Eden into the ravaged world. As in Weir's poem, there is a sense of finality: 'The world's great day is growing late', but here the end is contemplated with the calm that comes from having one foot in Eden. The world is choked with weeds, its fields filled with the crop of good and evil ready for harvest, but in Eden life still springs as new as on the first day. However, ultimately it is not Eden which offers hope. As in George Herbert's 'The Flower', the tree harvest springs from experience. There is no return to the garden, but the 'strange blessings' that we are offered have ripened in the tainted harvest of the world.

An increasing number of garden poems draw together the Eden imagery and the gardener. We still find an impetus towards poems about gardening stronger in America and Australia than in Britain, although they soon became increasingly prevalent everywhere. Among Robert Frost's many poems about gardening and husbandry, 'Putting in the Seed' encapsulates the movement from action and detail towards underlying truth. The poem directly echoes the experience of gardening; there is the simple everyday task, and through it the passionate response to the earth: 'How Love burns through the putting in the Seed'. Language has created as little distance as possible. There is no stepping back to view the garden, there is only the experience of living within it. The colloquial tone, directed at another person, and the deceptively self-effacing rhythm, minimise the effect of the poem as a literary device, although in fact the words are handled with a quiet skill that allows passion to be expressed without a trace of sentiment.

Mary Ursula Bethell's 'Time' relates the old idea of Time the destroyer to the experience of the gardener. We are taken swiftly from the instructive tone of 'Established is a good word, much used in garden books' to the intense expression of hope, even when the gardener knows that time will take away everything. The rhythm quickens, then slows to a meditative tone, as mortality is accepted, and foreseen. Basil Dowling's 'Scything' makes a similar leap from doing to knowing. The experience of the man scything at once conjures up and revokes the symbol of Time. Time is himself the scyther, and yet the man scything is timeless, an

> Emblem of an ancient time
> When wandering man first dreamed of home.

However, Time prevails; what seemed unchanging had a beginning and will have an end. The poet becomes Adam expelled from Eden, a representative of the human condition.

The marriage of the gardener and the Eden image proved fruitful to other poets. Martin Bell compresses the idea into a quatrain, in which the imperfect human harvest produced the 'unfriendly flowers', an outward result that seems not to correspond with the labour of love which proceeds from 'the garden of the heart'. Robert Graves' 'Gardener', one of his numerous garden poems, picks up the gardener's imperfections more prosaically, and contrasts them to the same man's vision of inner life within the garden. In spite of his self-deprecation, with which the ironic condescension of the poet appears to agree, the gardener's conception of angelic favour is clearly real. Only through such divine assistance could the clumsy and confused gardener 'bring the most to pass'.

Christopher Caudwell's gardener, on the other hand, is unredeemable. He is like Blake's priests in the Garden of Experience, crushing and inhibiting any manifestation of spontaneous life. Sexuality is denied, and even the lichen is scraped agonisingly off the walls, which must be kept devoid of life or growth. The Figure of the last verse, who used to walk in the garden in the cool of the day, as God did in Eden, turns out to be the devil, or Pan, with his hairy toes, who we now see as the god of life. Interestingly, this garden of desolation is, as the title tells us, a metaphor for the state of contemporary poetry.

Taner Bayber's poem, 'Corners of a Circle' sets the germinating flower seeds in the context of the newspapers reporting calamities, that line the seed trays. Yet, although the connection with inner life may be brittle, it is that connection which prevails, in the image of cloud and water touching earth. Dom Moraes' 'Gardener' dwells upon the sterile harvest that negates all dreams of beauty, and the futile labour of the gardener. Real understanding of the garden finally comes through begetting and experiencing the birth of his own child. Only then does the gardener become part of the rhythm of life himself, and is at last able to touch and know the trees. Marge Piercy's garden poem, however, takes the process of knowing right back into gardening itself. The gardener, in imitating the way that nature works, falling into the time rhythms of the garden, imposing nothing, ends by knowing herself, and faithfully anticipating a wholesome harvest of her own. In this poem, the paradox is for once resolved, and the gardener is integrated into an Eden of her own, which encompasses the entire cycle of nature.

We begin to see that in the twentieth century the garden image has taken on new meanings, as the Eden without has been so rapidly destroyed, possibly forever. Muir's note of finality is echoed in other poems. The old idea of the garden as a retreat, apart from the outside world, has evolved into an image of the garden as the only place left where human beings can interact with nature in a state of peace and harmony. The garden of the imagination and the garden of innocence have both come to represent the lost world of nature, from which poets could once draw unending inspiration. Not only poets, but also gardeners, have expressed the new significance of the garden. Wild gardens have become the deliberate re-creation of wilderness, organic gardens have become oases of unpolluted and undistorted natural cycles. Increasingly, gardens are becoming places not merely of conservation, but also environments where people can regain some awareness of the natural world that has been almost irretrievably eroded. Gardens of all types and sizes have become places apart from a damaged world. They are often designed precisely to draw our attention back to the natural world that our culture has sacrificed. Like all conceptions of nature this one reflects the viewpoint of its time. It is a pathetic image, because it is necessarily nostalgic and retrospective, However, such gardens become precious as places of regeneration and repose; they serve to heal the wounds that self-destruction inflicts. The moment in the garden has become poignant against a background of the end of the world as paradise.

Eliot's 'Four Quartets' takes us through the garden into the world of spirit which it contains. The moment in the rose garden expands into an apprehension of the regenerative life that is always just out of reach and out of sight, then goes beyond that to face the old question of time. But time here is no longer the potent enemy with the scythe, but is set against the immortal moment, which is always present.

As far as the garden image goes, it often appears to be sharpened by the cataclysmic context in which Eden must now be taken. The moment is all-important, because we now have to conceive that there may be nothing else. Eden has to be here and now or it is gone forever. The way into the garden is an existing route to connection with nature. Nature and the source of poetic inspiration have been intertwined for so long that we immediately recognise the parallel. The garden becomes a catalyst for new growth, and new images.

Robert Garioch's 'In Princes Street Gairdens' is almost a garden poem in spite of itself. The shop-folk and weill-daean tredsmen are only just up the street. The garden is scattered with human debris: band-stands, sculptures and graffiti, and yet it still offers retreat:

Jist you and me, a dou, and a wee cock-sparrie.

It isn't much, and the ironic understatement makes it seem less, and yet the garden provides space enough to look at it, and perceive some kind of pattern. Auden's 'Their Lonely Betters' considers lan-guage as the means by which humans have fallen, or become separated from the simple truths of nature. Again, the poem is ironic in tone, seeming to glance at nature with half an eye, like Beaumont contem-plating his merciless Eden, knowing that in fact it has nothing left to offer. Eden has been outgrown. Freda Downie's 'Her Garden' goes further. The garden is invaded and corrupted, besieged by the sterile and oppressive images without. Her grandmother's garden becomes 'five feet of bitterness', the plants themselves 'sour as social justice'. There is no escape from evil here. Later, Lauris Edmond, in 'Jardin des Columbieres' looks back into the lost garden of innocence, in this case childhood, but then goes on to realise that the garden has now become a symbol of property and profit. There is a turnstile at the gate, and it costs six francs to enter. Again, we feel the shadow cast by the black gowns of Blake's priests.

The latter poems regard Eden as lost or dead; Garioch's poem is ambiguous. The world impinges, but the moment in the garden does happen. In other poems, the garden triumphs, but only in the present, which expands into a bright vision, something beyond time. Stevie Smith's 'O grateful colours, bright looks!' catches the colours and events of a moment, in an urgent rhythm which suggests the seizing of simple signs of rightness while they are there. The demand is insistent:

Men!

Seize colours quick, heap them up while you can.

There is no promise of more than what the moment offers, but even a brief image of life does raise the question that perhaps this is not all.

Medbh Mcguckian's garden is a retreat filled with childhood images, treated with a light irony that finally brings them alive and undiminished into an adult world. She skilfully retains Eden, evading sentimentality by ironic recognition that the childhood world has been transposed to something suggestively sinister. Innocence has become experience, and Bunny in his white cotton nightcap is not dead, but potently adult.

The garden becomes one place where experience can be reflected truthfully. If nature is denied, both in the outer world and in human emotions, the one place where it can be acknowledged becomes, sometimes explicitly, sacred. In David Gascoigne's 'Winter Garden', the park, quiet and purified by the past tempest, becomes a reflection of the calm that could be reached after emotional storm. The silent gardeners have strewn the churned up paths with ash, and the garden is suspended in a moment between the cessation of storm and the onset of spring. The restless stranger cannot be part of this state of calm, but there is hope for him, as he has been drawn to it. The garden offers a mirror for exhausted emotion, a promise of some kind of repose.

Sylvia Plath's 'The Manor Garden' also puts destructive human emotion within the context of the garden. Here, the garden faithfully reflects the death and negation within. History is responsible for the broken stonework and neglected plants. The brutal images of the third verse, the 'two suicides' followed by 'hard stars', take us into a world where nature itself has become hostile. And yet in the last lines

The small birds converge, converge
With their gifts to a difficult borning.

There is some kind of hope, though barely acknowledged.

Elizabeth Jennings' 'Agony in any Garden' recalls Christ's agony in Gethsemane, and shows it to be the same as all passion and hopelessness. Any garden can be Gethsemane, and in her other garden poems, Jennings develops the garden image as a reflection of the whole of human experience and emotion. In this poem she states specifically that the garden is what we choose to make it. Elsewhere she considers the garden as art, which mirrors the world that we create. Whatever we make of it, however insignificant it may appear, it is vitally important.

Thom Gunn's 'The Garden of the Gods' takes us back into the garden itself for regeneration, seeing it not as a mirror, so much as a path into knowledge of the whole in which the individual is a part. His garden is full of movement, following paths to different places, coming and going, until in the fourth verse there is a pause in the rhythm:

It was sufficient there, to be.

At this point the garden expands into a vision that encompasses time, through the silent generations to the place of birth of the garden itself. The knowledge infuses the poet's being, as he traces the route back to Eden from awareness of his own body, rooted as it is in the knowledge of the earth.

Finally, the poem by Louis MacNeice captures the moment of immortality, and sets it against the inexorable advance of experience, which kills the moment and offers no reprieve. He sees the end approaching, that Eden is doomed, and humanity along with it, 'We are dying, Egypt, dying'. Yet simultaneously he reiterates that the moment is all. The garden offers no hope for the future, only the experience of the eternal present:

> And not expecting pardon,
> Hardened in heart anew,
> But glad to have sat under
> Thunder and rain with you,
> And grateful too
> For sunlight on the garden.

OBVIOUSLY it is harder to gain an overall perspective on contemporary garden poems because we do not yet have the overview of hindsight. Paradoxically, the hope that much garden poetry offers is the emphasis on the present. The garden is immediate, tangible, and actual; so the moments in the garden presented to us by the poets are the moments of insight that give meaning to the here and now. We began with the connections between the gardens and the poems: the garden as both image and source of inspiration. Looking at them through the centuries, we have seen how both gardens and poems reflect a composite image of their own particular time. Through this double image we gain perspective on historical change, in terms of language, poetic form, perception of nature and the human relationship to it. We also see how the poet's individual vision asserts itself within the framework of time and place. As we draw closer to the present, the spectrum of place widens and we find the poems also coming from Canada, America, Australia, New Zealand and elsewhere.

It is interesting to consider a poem in the context of particular place or time, but the poem itself, if it succeeds, will transcend its background. The garden poems move from the actual, specific experience of the garden to a wider, more universal, but also unique, vision.
A poem separated from our experience by five centuries, or half
a world, loses none of its immediacy if we can still respond to
the experience of the poet. Every poem was written in the
present, and is read in the present, just as the moment
in the garden, as Eliot shows us, is always now.

The Poems

The Meaning of Charity

'It is a ful trie tree', quod he, 'trewely to telle. *precious*
root Mercy is the more therof; the myddul stok is ruthe; *stem* *pity*
The leves ben lele wordes, the lawe of holy chirche;
humble The blosmes beth buxom speche and benigne lokynge. *looks*
is called Pacience hatte the pure tree and pouere symple of herte, *poverty*
through And so thorough god and goode men groweth
the fruyt Charite.'
'I wolde travaille', quod I, 'this tree to se twenty
hundred myle,
And to have my fulle of that fruyt forsake al
other saulee. *food*
Lord!' quod I, 'if any wight wite whiderout it groweth?' *man knows*
'It groweth in a gardyn', quod he, 'that god
made hymselve
Amyddes mannes body; the more is of that stokke. *springs from man's body*
Herte highte the herber that it Inne groweth, *soil*
free will And *liberum arbitrium* hath the lond to ferme,
Under Piers the Plowman to piken it and weden it.' *hoe*

27

Description of a Garden
FROM 'THE PARLIAMENT OF FOWLS'

A gardyn saw I ful of blosmy bowes
Upon a ryver, in a grene mede,
There as swetnesse everemore inow is,
With floures white, blewe, yelwe, and rede,
And colde welle-stremes, nothyng dede,
That swymmen ful of smale fishes lighte,
With fynnes rede and skales sylver bryghte.

On every bow the bryddes herde I synge,   *birds*
With voys of aungel in here armonye;   *their*
Some besyede hem here bryddes forth to brynge;
The litel conyes to here pley gonne hye;   *made haste*
And ferther al aboute I gan aspye
The dredful ro, the buk, the hert and hynde,   *timid*
Squyrels, and bestes smale of gentil kynde.

Of instruments of strenges in acord
Herde I so pleye a ravyshyng swetnesse,
That God, that makere is of al and lord,
Ne herde nevere beter, as I gesse.
Therwith a wynd, unnethe it myghte be lesse,   *hardly*
Made in the leves grene a noyse softe
Acordaunt to the foules song alofte.   *in harmony with*

Th'air of that place so attempre was   *mild*
That nevere was ther grevaunce of hot ne cold;
There wex ek every holsom spice and gras;
No man may there waxe sek ne old;   *also grew*
Yet was there joye more a thousandfold
Than man can telle; ne nevere wolde it nyghte,
But ay cler day to any manes syghte.

The Rose

FROM 'THE ROMAUNT OF THE ROSE'

In thilke mirrour saw I tho,
Among a thousand thinges mo,
rosebush   A roser chargid full of rosis,
That with an hegge aboute enclos is.
Tho had I sich lust and envie,
That for Parys ne for Pavie   *Pavia*
Nolde I have left to goon and see   *would I have neglected to*
There grettist hep of roses be
Whanne I was with this rage hent,   *seized*
That caught hath many a man and shent,   *ruined*
Toward the roser gan I go;
And whanne I was not fer therfro,
The savour of the roses swote   *sweet*
Me smot right to the herte-rote,
As I hadde all enbawmed be.
And if I ne hadde endouted me   *feared*
To have ben hatid or assailed,
My thankis, wolde I not have failed
To pulle a rose of all that route   *company*
To beren in myn hond aboute,
And smellen to it where I wente;
But ever I dredde me to repente,
And lest it grevede or forthoughte   *displeased*
The lord that thilke gardyn wroughte.
Of roses ther were gret won;
So faire waxe never in ron.   *bush*
buds   Of knoppes clos some sawe I there;
And some wel beter woxen were;
And some ther ben of other moysoun,   *crop*
That drowe nygh to her sesoun,
And spedde hem faste for to sprede.
I love well sich roses rede,
For brode roses and open also
Ben passed in a day or two;
But knoppes wille al freshe be
Two dayes, atte leest, or thre.
The knoppes gretly liked me,
For fairer may ther no man se.
Whoso myght have oon of alle,
It ought hym ben full lief withalle.   *he should like*
Might I a gerlond of hem geten,
For no richesse I wolde it leten.   *let go*

Among the knoppes I ches oon
So fair, that of the remenaunt noon
Ne preise I half so well as it,
consider Whanne I avise it in my wit. *mind*
For it so well was enlumyned
With colour reed and as well fyned
As nature couthe it make faire. *knows how*
And it hath leves wel foure paire,
nature That Kynde hath sett, thorough his knowyng,
Aboute the rede Rose spryngyng.
The stalke was as rishe right, *upright as a rush*
And theron stod the knoppe upright,
That it ne bowide upon no side.
The swote smelle sprong so wide
That it dide all the place aboute—

JAMES I OF SCOTLAND   1394–1437

The Garden
FROM 'THE KINGIS QUAIR'

Now was there maid fast by the touris wall *tower*
rdyn faire, and in the cornere set
arbour Ane herbere grene, with wandis long and small *rods*
Railit about; and so with treis set
Was all the place, and hawthorn hegis knet,
person That lyf was none, was walking there forby, *past*
That myght within scarse ony wight aspye. *hardly*

boughs So thik the bewis and the leves grene
Beschadit all the aleyes that there were;
And myddis of the herbere myght be sene
The scharp, grene, swetë jenipere,
Growing so faire with branchis here and there,
That, as it semyt to a lyf without,
The bewis spred the herbere all about.

And on the small grene twistis sat *twigs*
The lytill swete nyghtingale and song,
So loud and clere, the ympnis consecrat *hymns*
Off lufis use, now soft, now lowd among,
That all the gardyng and the wallis rong
Ryght of their song, and of the copill next *couple*
Off thaire swete armony, and lo the text:

30

'Worschippe, ye that loveris bene this May,
For of your blisse the kalendis ar begonne,   *first days*
And sing with us, away winter, away!
Cum somer, cum, the swete sesoune and sonne!
Awake, for schame, that have your hevynnis wonne,
And amorously lift up your hedis all.
Thank lufe that list yow to his merci call.'   *calls whomever he pleases*

       *   *   *

And therewith kest I doune myn eye ageyne
Quhare as I saw walking under the toure,
Fill secretly new cummyn hir to pleyne,   *to amuse himself*
The fairest or the freschest yong floure
That ever I sawe, me thought, before that houre;
For quhich sodayne abate anone astert   *shock*
The blude of all my body to my hert.

abashed And though I stude abaisit tho alyte,   *a little*
No wonder was, for quhy my wittis all
Were so ouercome with plesance and delyte,
Onely throu latting of myn eyen fall,
That sudaynly my hert become hir thrall
For ever of free wyll, for of manace
There was no takyn in hir swetë face.   *sign*

And in my hede I drewe ryght hastily,
And eftsones I lent it forth ageyne
And sawe hir walk, that verray womanly,
With no wight mo bot onely women tweyne.   *two*
Than gan I studye in my self and seyne:
'A, swete, ar ye a warldly creature,
Or hevinly thing in liknesse of nature?

Or ar ye god Cupidis owin princesse,
And cummyn are to lowse me out of band?   *fetters*
Or ar ye verray Nature the goddesse,
That have depaynted with your hevinly hand
This gardyn full of flouris as they stand?
Quhat sall I think? Allace, quhat reverence
Sall I minister to your excellence?

Gif ye a goddesse be and that ye like
To do me payne, I may it nought astert.   *escape*
Gif ye be warldly wight that dooth me sike,   *sigh*
Quhy lest god mak you so, my derrest hert,
helpless To do a sely presoner thus smert,
That lufis, yow all, and wote of nought bot wo?
And therefore, merci, swete, sen it is so.'

I have a newe garden

I have a newe garden,
And newe is begunne:
Swich another garden
Know I not under sunne.

In the middes of my garden
Is a peryr set,   *pear tree*
And it wille non per bern   *bear no pear*
But a per Jenet.   *early pear*

The fairest maide of this town
Preyed me
For to griffen her a grif   *graft her a short*
Of mine pery tree.

Whan I hadde hem griffed,
Alle at her wille,
The win and the ale
She dede in fille.   *with wine and ale*

And I griffed her
Right up in her home: .
And by that day twenty wowkes   *weeks*
It was quik in her womb.

That day twelfus month
That maide I met:
She seid it was a per Robert
But non per Jonet!

Sweit rois of vertew

Sweit rois of vertew and of gentilnes,
Delitsum lilye of everye lustines,   *all youthful vigour*
Richest in bontye and in bewtye cleir,
And everye vertew that is held most deir—
Except, onlye, that ye ar mercyles.

Into your garthe, this day, I did persew :   *go*
Thair saw I flowres that freshe wer of hew;
Baith white and reid moist lusty wer to seine,   *pleasant*
And halsum herbes upone stalkes grene—
Yit leif nor flowr find could I nane of rew.

fear I dout that Merche with his caild blastes keine
Hes slane this gentill herbe that I of mene,   *make a plea to*
Whois petewous deithe dois to my hart sic pane
make poetry That I wald mak to plant his rute agane,
comforting So confortand his leves unto me bene.

This day day dawes

This day day dawes,   *dawns*
This gentil day day dawes,
This gentil day dawes,
And I must home gone.
This gentil day dawes,
This day day dawes,
This gentil day dawes,
And we must home gone.

In a glorius garden grene
Sawe I sitting a comly quene
Among the floures that fresh bene.
She gaderd a floure and set betwene.
The lily-whighte rose me thought I sawe,
The lily-whighte rose me thought I sawe,
And ever she sang:

In that garden be floures of hewe,   *colour*
gillyflower   The gelofir gent that she well knewe;   *pretty*
The floure-de-luce she did on rewe,   *had pity on*
And said, 'The white rose is most trewe
This garden to rule by rightwis lawe.'
The lily-whighte rose me thought I sawe,
And ever she sang:

The Gardener

The gardener stands in his bower door
    With a primrose in his hand;
And by there came a true maiden
    As slim as a willow wand.

'O lady, can you fancy me
    And will you be my bride!
You shall have all the flowers in my garden
    To be to you a weed. *dress*

'The lily white to be your smock,
    It becomes your body best;
Your head shall be dressed with gillyflower
    With the red rose in your breast.

'Your gown shall be the sweet william,
    Your coat the camovine,
Your apron of the salads neat
    That taste both sweet and fine.

'Your gloves shall be the marigold
    All glittering to your hand;
Well dropped o'er with blue blaewort
    That grows among corn land.'

'Young man, you've shaped a weed for me
    Among your summer flowers!
Now I will shape another for you
    Among the winter showers.

'The new-fall'n snow to be your smock,
    It becomes your body best;
Your head shall be wrapped with the eastern wind
    And the cold rain on your breast.'

Inscription in a Garden

If any flower that here is grown
   Or any herb may ease your pain,
Take and accompt it as your own,
   But recompense the like again;
     For some and some is honest play,
     And so my wife taught me to say.

If here to walk you take delight,
   Why, come and welcome when you will;
If I bid you sup here this night,
   Bid me another time, and still
     Think some and some is honest play,
     For so my wife taught me to say.

Thus if you sup or dine with me,
   If you walk here or sit at ease,
If you desire the thing you see,
   And have the same your mind to please,
     Think some and some is honest play,
     And so my wife taught me to say.

In Youth is Pleasure

In a herber green, asleep where I lay,
The birds sang sweet in the mids of the day;
I dreamèd fast of mirth and play.
   In youth is pleasure, in youth is pleasure.

Methought I walked still to and fro,
And from her company could not go;
But when I waked it was not so.
   In youth is pleasure, in youth is pleasure.

Therefore my heart is surely pight
Of her alone to have a sight,
Which is my joy and heart's delight.
   In youth is pleasure, in youth is pleasure.

The Gardin of Adonis
FROM 'THE FAERIE QUEENE'

In that same Gardin all the goodly flowres,
  Wherewith dame Nature doth her beautifie,
  And decks the girlonds of her paramoures,
  Are fetcht: there is the first seminarie
  Of all things, that are borne to liue and die,
  According to their kindes. Long worke it were,
  Here to account the endlesse progenie
  Of all the weedes, that bud and blossome there;
But so much as doth need, must needs be counted here.

It sited was in fruitfull soyle of old,
  And girt in with two walles on either side;
  The one of yron, the other of bright gold,
  That none might thorough breake, nor ouer-stride:
  And double gates it had, which opened wide,
  By which both in and out men moten pas;
  Th'one faire and fresh, the other old and dride:
  Old *Genius* the porter of them was,
Old *Genius*, the which a double nature has.

He letteth in, he letteth out to wend,
  All that to come into the world desire;
  A thousand thousand naked babes attend
  About him day and night, which doe require,
  That he with fleshly weedes would them attire:
  Such as him list, such as eternall fate
  Ordained hath, he clothes with sinfull mire,
  And sendeth forth to liue in mortall state,
Till they againe returne backe by the hinder gate.

After that they againe returned beene,
  They in that Gardin planted be againe;
  And grow afresh, as they had neuer seene
  Fleshly corruption, nor mortall paine.
  Some thousand yeares so doen they there remaine;
  And then of him are clad with other hew,
  Or sent into the chaungefull world againe,
  Till thither they returne, where first they grew:
So like a wheele around they runne from old to new.

The substance is not chaunged, nor altered,
   But th'only forme and outward fashion;
   For euery substance is conditioned
   To change her hew, and sundry formes to don,
   Meet for her temper and complexion:
   For formes are variable and decay,
   By course of kind, and by occasion;
   And that faire flowre of beautie fades away,
As doth the lilly fresh before the sunny ray.

Great enimy to it, and to all the rest,
   That in the *Gardin* of *Adonis* springs,
   Is wicked *Time*, who with his scyth addrest,
   Does mow the flowring herbes and goodly things,
   And all their glory to the ground downe flings,
   Where they doe wither, and are fowly mard:
   He flyes about, and with his flaggy wings
   Beates downe both leaues and buds without regard,
Ne euer pittie may relent his malice hard.

Yet pittie often did the gods relent,
   To see so faire things mard, and spoyled quight:
   And their great mother *Venus* did lament
   The losse of her deare brood, her deare delight:
   Her hart was pierst with pittie at the sight,
   When walking through the Gardin, them she spyde,
   Yet no'te she find redresse for such despight.
   For all that liues, is subiect to that law:
All things decay in time, and to their end do draw.

But were it not, that *Time* their troubler is,
   All that in this delightfull Gardin growes,
   Should happie be, and haue immortall blis:
   For here all plentie, and all pleasure flowes,
   And sweet loue gentle fits emongst them throwes,
   Without fell rancor, or fond gealosie;
   Franckly each paramour his leman knowes,
   Each bird his mate, ne any does enuie
Their goodly meriment, and gay felicitie.

Nymph of the gard'n

Nymph of the gard'n, where all beauties be:
    Beauties which do in excellencie passe
    His who till death lookt in a watrie glasse
Or hers whom naked the Trojan boy did see.
Sweet gard'n Nymph, which keeps the Cherrie tree,
    Whose fruit dothe farre th'Esperian taste surpass:
    Most sweet-faire, most faire-sweet, do not alas,
From comming neare those Cherries banish me:
    For though full of desire, emptie of wit,
Admitted late by your best-graced grace,
I caught at one of them a hungrie bit;
Pardon that fault, once more graunt me the place,
    And I do sweare even by the same delight,
    I will but kisse, I never more will bite.

Of his mistress
upon occasion of her walking in a garden

My lady's presence makes the roses red,
Because to see her lips they blush for shame:
The lily's leaves, for envy, pale became,
And her white hands in them this envy bred.
The marigold abroad her leaves doth spread,
Because the sun's and her power is the same;
The violet of purple colour came,
Dyed with the blood she made my heart to shed.
In brief, all flowers from her their virtue take:
From her sweet breath their sweet smells do proceed,
The living heat which her eye-beams do make
Warmeth the ground, and quickeneth the seed.
The rain wherewith she watereth these flowers
Falls from mine eyes, which she dissolves in showers.

Down in a Garden

Down in a garden sat my dearest Love,
Her skin more soft and white than down of swan,
More tender-hearted than the turtle-dove,
And far more kind than bleeding pelican.
I courted her; she rose and blushing said,
'Why was I born to live and die a maid?'
With that I plucked a pretty marigold,
Whose dewy leaves shut up when day is done:
'Sweeting,' I said, 'arise, look and behold,
A pretty riddle I'll to thee unfold:
These leaves shut in as close as cloistered nun,
Yet will they open when they see the sun.'
'What mean you by this riddle, sir?' she said,
'I pray expound it.' Then I thus began:
'Know maids are made for men, man for a maid.'
With that she changed her colour and grew wan:
'Since that this riddle you so well unfold,
Be you the sun, I'll be the marigold.'

The Garden

The world's a garden; pleasures are the flowers,
    Of fairest hues, in form and number many:
    The lily, first, pure-whitest flower of any,
Rose sweetest rare, with pinkèd gilliflowers,
The violet, and double marigold,
    And pansy too: but after all mischances,
Death's winter comes and kills with sudden cold
    Rose, lily, violet, marigold, pink, pansies.

From you have I been absent in the spring

From you have I been absent in the spring,
    When proud pied April, dressed in all his trim,
Hath put a spirit of youth in every thing,
    That heavy Saturn laughed and leaped with him.
Yet nor the lays of birds, nor the sweet smell
    Of different flowers in odour and in hue,
Could make me any summer's story tell,
    Or from their proud lap pluck them
                                   where they grew:
Nor did I wonder at the lily's white,
    Nor praise the deep vermilion in the rose;
They were but sweet, but figures of delight,
    Drawn after you, you pattern of all those.
        Yet seemed it winter still, and, you away,
        As with your shadow I with these did play.

The Duke of York's Garden
FROM 'RICHARD II'

Gardener. Go, bind thou up yond dangling apricocks,
Which, like unruly children, make their sire
Stoop with oppression of their prodigal weight:
Give some supportance to the bending twigs.—
Go thou, and like an executioner
Cut off the heads of too-fast growing sprays,
That look too lofty in our commonwealth.
All must be even in our government.—
You thus employ'd, I will go root away
The noisome weeds, that without profit suck
The soil's fertility from wholesome flowers.
    Servant. Why should we in the compass of a pale
Keep law and form and due proportion,
Showing, as in a model, our firm estate,
When our sea-walled garden, the whole land,
Is full of weeds, her fairest flowers chok'd up,
Her fruit-trees all unprun'd, her hedges ruin'd,
Her knots disorder'd, and her wholesome herbs
Swarming with caterpillars?
    Gardener.   Hold thy peace.
He that hath suffer'd this disorder'd spring
Hath now himself met with the fall of leaf:
The weeds that his broad-spreading leaves did shelter
That seem'd in eating him to hold him up,
Are pluck'd up root and all by Bolingbroke;
I mean the Earl of Wiltshire, Bushy, Green.
    Servant. What! are they dead?
    Gardener.   They are;
                                        and Bolingbroke
Hath seiz'd the wasteful king.—O! what pity is it
That he had not so trimm'd and dress'd his land
As we this garden! We at time of year
Do wound the bark, the skin of our fruit-trees,
Lest, being over-proud in sap and blood,
With too much riches it confound itself:
Had he done so to great and growing men,
They might have liv'd to bear, and he to taste
Their fruits of duty. Superfluous branches
We lop away, that bearing boughs may live:
Had he done so, himself had borne the crown,
Which waste of idle hours hath quite thrown down.

A Lawn before a Shepherd's Cottage
FROM 'THE WINTER'S TALE'

Perdita. Sir, the year growing ancient,—
Not yet on summer's death, nor on the birth
Of trembling winter,—the fairest flowers o' the season
Are our carnations, and streak'd gillyvors,
Which some call nature's bastards : of that kind
Our rustic garden's barren, and I care not
To get slips of them.
    Polixenes.   Wherefore, gentle maiden,
Do you neglect them?
    Perdita.   For I have heard it said
There is an art which in their piedness, shares
With great creating nature.
    Polixenes.   Say there be;
Yet nature is made better by no mean,
But nature makes that mean : so, o'er that art,
Which you say adds to nature, is an art
That nature makes. You see, sweet maid, we marry
A gentler scion to the wildest stock,
And make conceive a bark of baser kind
By bud of nobler race : this is an art
Which does mend nature,—change it rather; but
The art itself is nature.
    Perdita.   So it is.
    Polixenes. Then make your garden rich in gillyvors,
And do not call them bastards.
    Perdita.   I'll not put
The dibble in earth to set one slip of them :
No more than were I painted I would wish
This youth should say 't were well, and only therefore
Desire to breed by me.—Here's flowers for you;
Hot lavender, mints, savory, marjoram;
The marigold, that goes to bed wi' the sun
And with him rises weeping : these are flowers
Of middle summer and I think they are given
To men of middle age. You are very welcome.

There is a Garden in her face

There is a Garden in her face,
Where Roses and white Lillies grow;
A heav'nly paradice is that place,
Wherein all pleasant fruits doe flow.
   There Cherries grow, which none may buy
   Till Cherry ripe themselves doe cry.

Those Cherries fayrely doe enclose
Of Orient Pearle a double row,
   Which when her lovely laughter showes,
They looke like Rose-buds fill'd with snow.
   Yet them nor Peere nor Prince can buy,
   Till Cherry ripe themselves doe cry.

Her Eyes like Angels watch them still;
Her Browes like bended bowes doe stand,
   Threatning with piercing frownes to kill
All that attempt with eye or hand
   Those sacred Cherries to come nigh,
   Till Cherry ripe themselves doe cry.

Genesis, ch.2, v.8–10; ch.3, v.8–12

And the LORD God planted a garden eastward in Eden; and there he put the man whom he had formed.

And out of the ground made the LORD God to grow every tree that is pleasant to the sight, and good for food; the tree of life also in the midst of the garden, and the tree of knowledge of good and evil.

And a river went out of Eden to water the garden; and from thence it was parted, and became into four heads.

*   *   *

And they heard the voice of the LORD GOD walking in the garden in the cool of the day : and Adam and his wife hid themselves from the presence of the LORD GOD amongst the trees of the garden.

And the LORD GOD called unto Adam, and said unto him, Where art thou?

And he said, I heard thy voice in the garden, and I was afraid, because I was naked; and I hid myself.

And he said, Who told thee that thou wast naked? Hast thou eaten of the tree, whereof I commanded thee that thou shouldest not eat?

And the man said, The woman whom thou gavest to be with me, she gave me of the tree, and I did eat.

Song of Solomon Ch.4, v.12–16

A garden inclosed *is* my sister, *my* spouse; a spring shut up, a fountain sealed.

Thy plants are an orchard of pomegranates, with pleasant fruits; camphire, with spikenard,

Spikenard and saffron; calamus and cinnamon, with all trees of frankincense: myrrh and aloes, with all the chief spices:

A fountain of gardens, a well of living waters, and streams from Lebanon.

Awake, O north wind; and come, thou south; blow upon my garden, that the spices thereof may flow out. Let my beloved come into his garden, and eat his pleasant fruits.

BEN JONSON   1572–1637

Then hath thy orchard fruit
FROM 'TO PENSHURST'

Then hath thy orchard fruit, thy garden flowers,
    Fresh as the ayre, and new as are the houres.
The early cherry, with the later plum,
    Fig, grape, and quince, each in his time doth come;
The blushing apricot, and woolly peach
    Hang on thy walls, that every child may reach.
And though thy walls be of the countrey stone,
    They are rear'd with no mans ruine, no mans grone,
There's none, that dwell about them, wish them downe;
    But all come in, the farmer, and the clowne:
And no one empty-handed, to salute
    Thy lord, and lady, though they have no sute.

Twicknam Garden

Blasted with sighs, and surrounded with tears,
  Hither I come to seek the spring,
  And at mine eyes, and at mine ears,
Receive such balms, as else cure everything;
  But O, self traitor, I do bring
The spider love, which transubstantiates all,
  And can convert manna to gall,
And that this place may thoroughly be thought
  True paradise, I have the serpent brought.

'Twere wholesomer for me, that winter did
  Benight the glory of this place,
  And that a grave frost did forbid
These trees to laugh, and mock me to my face;
  But that I may not this disgrace
Endure, nor yet leave loving, Love, let me
  Some senseless piece of this place be;
Make me a mandrake, so I may groan here,
  Or a stone fountain weeping out my year.

Hither with crystal vials, lovers come,
  And take my tears, which are love's wine,
And try your mistress' tears at home,
For all are false, that taste not just like mine;
  Alas, hearts do not in eyes shine,
Nor can you more judge woman's thoughts by tears,
  Than by her shadow, what she wears.
O perverse sex, where none is true but she,
  Who's therefore true, because her truth kills me.

Daphnis to Ganymede

If thou wilt come and dwell with me at home,
My sheep-cote shall be strowed with new green rushes;
We'll haunt the trembling prickets as they roam
About the fields, along the hawthorn bushes:
  I have a piebald cur to hunt the hare:
  So we will live with dainty forest fare.

Nay, more than this, I have a garden plot,
Wherein there wants nor herbs, nor roots,
                                nor flowers,—
Flowers to smell, roots to eat, herbs for the pot,—
And dainty shelters when the welkin lours:
  Sweet smelling beds of lilies and of roses,
  Which rosemary banks and lavender encloses.

There grows the gillyflower, the mint, the daisy
Both red and white, the blue-veined violet,
The purple hyacinth, the spike to please thee,
The scarlet-dyed carnation bleeding yet,
  The sage, the savory, the sweet marjoram,
  Hyssop, thyme, and eye-bright, good for the
                              blind and dumb;

The pink, the primrose, cowslip, and daffadilly,
The harebell blue, the crimson columbine,
Sage, lettuce, parsley, and the milk-white lily,
The rose, and speckled flower called sops-in-wine,
  Fine pretty kingcups, and the yellow boots
  That grow by rivers, and by shallow brooks;

And many thousand more, I cannot name,
Of herbs and flowers that in gardens grow,
I have for thee; and conies that be tame,
Young rabbits, white as swan, and black as crow,
  Some speckled here and there with dainty spots;
  And more, I have two milch and milk-white goats.

And these, and more, I'll give thee for thy love,
If these, and more, may tice thy love away:
I have a pigeon-house, in it a dove,
Which I love more than mortal tongue can say;
  And, last of all, I'll give thee a little lamb
  To play withal, new weaned from her dam.

Like the Idalian Queen

Like the Idalian queen,
Her hair about her eyne,
With neck and breast's ripe apples to be seen,
At first glance of the morn,
In Cyprus' gardens gathering those fair flow'rs
Which of her blood were born,
I saw, but fainting saw, my paramours.
The Graces naked danc'd about the place,
The winds and trees amaz'd
With silence on her gaz'd;
The flow'rs did smile, like those upon her face,
And as their aspen stalks those fingers band,
That she might read my case,
A hyacinth I wish'd me in her hand.

A Meditation for his Mistresse

You are a *Tulip* seen to day,
But (Dearest) of so short a stay;
That where you grew, scarce man can say.

You are a love *July-flower*,
Yet one rude wind, or ruffling shower,
Will force you hence, (and in an houre.)

You are a sparkling *Rose* i'th'bud,
Yet lost, ere that chast flesh and blood
Can shew where you or grew, or stood.

You are a full-spread faire-set Vine,
And can with Tendrills love intwine,
Yet dry'd, ere you distill your Wine.

You are like Balme inclosed (well)
In *Amber*, or some *Chrystall* shell,
Yet lost ere you transfuse your smell.

You are a dainty *Violet*,
Yet wither'd, ere you can be set
Within the Virgins Coronet.

A Contemplation upon flowers

Brave flowers, that I could gallant it like you
And be as little vaine,
You come abroad, and make a harmelesse shew,
And to your beds of Earthe againe;
You are not proud, you know your birth
For your Embroiderd garments are from Earth:

You doe obey your months, and times, but I
Would have it ever spring,
My fate would know no winter, never die
Nor thinke of such a thing;
Oh that I could my bed of Earth but view
And Smile, and looke as Chearefully as you:

Oh teach me to see Death, and not to fear
But rather to take trucc;
How often have I seene you at a Bier,
And there look fresh and spruce,
You fragrant flowers, then teach me that my breath
Like yours may sweeten, and perfume my Death.

The Flower

How fresh, O Lord, how sweet and clean
Are thy returns! ev'n as the flowers in spring;
To which, besides their own demean,
The late-past frosts tributes of pleasure bring.
     Grief melts away
     Like snow in May,
As if there were no such cold thing.

Who would have thought my shrivel'd heart
Could have recover'd greennesse? It was gone
Quite under ground; as flowers depart
To see their mother-root, when they have blown;
     Where they together
     All the hard weather,
Dead to the world, keep house unknown.

These are thy wonders, Lord of power,
Killing and quickning, bringing down to hell
And up to heaven in an houre;
Making a chiming of a passing-bell.
     We say amisse,
     This or that is:
Thy word is all, if we could spell.

O that I once past changing were,
Fast in thy Paradise, where no flower can wither!
Many a spring I shoot up fair,
Offring at heav'n, growing and groning thither:
     Nor doth my flower
     Want a spring-showre,
My sinnes and I joining together.

But while I grow in a straight line,
Still upwards bent, as if heav'n were mine own,
Thy anger comes, and I decline:
What frost to that? what pole is not the zone,
     Where all things burn,
     When thou dost turn,
And the least frown of thine is shown?

And now in age I bud again,
After so many deaths I live and write;
I once more smell the dew and rain,
And relish versing: O my onely light,
     It cannot be
     That I am he
On whom thy tempests fell all night.

These are thy wonders, Lord of love,
To make us see we are but flowers that glide:
Which when we once can finde and prove,
Thou hast a garden for us, where to bide.
     Who would be more,
     Swelling through store,
Forfeit their Paradise by their pride.

JAMES SHIRLEY   1596–1666

The Garden

This Garden does not take my eyes,
Though here you shew how art of men
Can purchase Nature at a price
Would stock old Paradise agen.

These glories while you dote upon,
I envie not your Spring nor pride,
Nay boast the Summer all your own,
My thoughts with lesse are satisfied.

Give me a little plot of ground,
Where might I with the Sun agree,
Though every day he walk the Round,
My Garden he should seldom see.

Those Tulips that such wealth display,
To court my eye, shall lose their name,
Though now they listen, as if they
Expected I should praise their flame.

But I would see my self appear
Within the Violets drooping head,
On which a melancholy tear
The discontented Morne hath shed.

Within their buds let Roses sleep,
And virgin Lillies on their stemme,
Till sighes from Lovers glide, and creep
Into their leaves to open them.

I' th' Center of my ground compose
Of Bayes and Ewe my Summer room,
Which may so oft as I repose,
Present my Arbour, and my Tombe.

No woman here shall find me out,
Or if a chance do bring one hither,
I'll be secure, for round about
I'll moat it with my eyes foul weather.

No Bird shall live within my pale,
To charme me with their shames of Art,
Unlesse some wandring Nightingale
Come here to sing, and break her heart.

Upon whose death I'll try to write
An Epitaph in some funeral stone,
So sad, and true, it may invite
My self to die, and prove mine owne.

Paradise
FROM 'PARADISE LOST'

Another side, umbrageous Grots and Caves
Of coole recess, o'er which the mantling Vine
Layes forth her purple Grape, and gently creeps
Luxuriant; mean while murmuring waters fall
Down the slope hills, disperst, or in a Lake,
That to the fringed Bank with Myrtle crownd,
Her chrystall mirror holds, unite their streams.
The Birds thir quire apply; aires, vernal aires,
Breathing the smell of field and grove, attune
The trembling leaves, while Universal *Pan*
Knit with the *Graces* and the *Hours* in dance
Led on th' Eternal Sprig. Not that faire field
Of *Enna*, where *Proserpin* gathring flours
Her self a fairer Flowre by gloomie *Dis*
Was gatherd, which cost *Ceres* all that pain
To seek her through the world; nor that sweet Grove
Of *Daphne* by *Orontes*, and th' inspir'd
Castalian Spring might with this Paradise
Of *Eden* strive; nor that *Nyseian* Ile
Girt with the River *Triton*, where old *Cham*,
Whom Gentiles *Ammon* call and *Libyan Jove*,
Hid *Amalthea* and her Florid Son
Young *Bacchus* from his Stepdame *Rhea's* eye;
Nor where *Abassin* Kings thir issue Guard,
Mount *Amara*, though this by som suppos'd
True Paradise under the *Ethiop* Line
By *Nilus* head, enclos'd with shining Rock,
A whole dayes journey high, but wide remote
From this *Assyrian* Garden, where the Fiend
Saw undelighted all delight, all kind
Of living Creatures new to sight and strange:
Two of far nobler shape erect and tall,
Godlike erect, with native Honour clad
In naked Majestie seemd Lords of all,
And worthie seemd, for in thir looks Divine
The image of thir glorious Maker shon,
Truth, Wisdome, Sanctitude severe and pure,
Severe, but in true filial freedom plac't.

The Garden

The Garden's quit with me : as yesterday
I walked in that, to day that walks in me ;
   Through all my memorie
It sweetly wanders, and has found a way
  To make me honestly possess
   What still Anothers is.

Yet this Gains dainty sense doth gall my Minde
With the remembrance of a bitter Loss.
   Alas, how odd and cross
Are earths Delights, in which the Soule can finde
  No Honey, but withall some Sting
   To check the pleasing thing !

For now I'm haunted with the thought of that
Heavn-planted Garden, where felicitie
   Flourished on every Tree.
Lost, lost it is ; for at the guarded gate
  A flaming Sword forbiddeth Sin
   (That 's I,) to enter in.

O Paradise ! when I was turned out
Hadst thou but kept the Serpent still within,
   My banishment had been
Less sad and dangerous : but round about
  This wide world runneth rageing He
   To banish me from me :

I feel that through my soule he death hath shot ;
And thou, alas, hast locked up Lifes Tree.
   O Miserable Me,
What help were left, had JESUS's Pity not
  Shewd me another Tree, which can
   Enliven dying Man.

That Tree, made Fertile by his own dear blood ;
And by his Death with quickning virtue fraught.
   I now dread not the thought
O barracado'd Eden, since as good
  A Paradise I planted see
   On open Calvarie.

The Garden

Happy art Thou whom God does bless
  With the full choice of thine own Happiness;
  And happier yet, because thou'rt blest
  With prudence, how to choose the best:
In Books and Gardens thou hast plac'd aright
  (Things which thou well dost understand;
And both dost make with thy laborious hand)
  Thy noble, innocent delight:
And in thy virtuous Wife, where thou again dost meet
  Both pleasures more refined and sweet:
  The fairest Garden in her Looks,
  And in her Mind the wisest Books.
Oh, Who would change these soft, yet solid joys,
  For empty shows and senceless noyce;
  And all which rank Ambition breeds,
Which seem such beauteous Flowers, and are
                              such poisonous Weeds.

When God did Man to his own likeness make,
As much as Clay, though of the purest kind,
  By the great Potters are refin'd;
  Could the Divine Impression take,
  He thought it fit to place him, where
  A kind of Heaven too did appear,
As far as Earth could such a likeness bear:
  That man no happiness might want,
Which Earth to her first Master could afford;
  He did a Garden for him plant
By the quick hand of his Omnipotent Word.
As the chif Help and Joy of humane life,
He gave him the first Gift; first, ev'n before a Wife.

For God, the universal Architect,
  T'had been as easie to erect
A Louvre or Escurial, or a Tower
That might with Heav'n communication hold,
As Babel vainly thought to do of old:
  He wanted not the skill or power,
  In the World's Fabrick those were shown,
And the Materials were all his own,
But well he knew what place would best agree
With Innocence, and with Felicity:
And we elsewhere still seek for them in vain,
If any part of either yet remain;
If any part of either we expect,
This may our Judgment in the search direct;
God the first Garden made, and the first City, Cain,

Oh blessed shades! O gentle cool retreat
    From all th'immoderate Heat,
In which the frantick World does burn and sweat!
This does the Lion-Star, Ambitions rage;
This Avarice, the Dog-stars Thirst asswage;
Every where else their fatal power we see,
They make and rule Mans wretched Destiny:
    They neither Set, nor disappear,
    But tyranize o'r all the Year;
Whilst we ne'r feel their Flame or Influence here.
    The Birds that dance from bough to bough,
    And sing above in every Tree,
    Are not from Fears and Cares more free,
Then we who Lie, or Walk below,
    And should by right be Singers too.

What Princes Quire of Musick can excell
    That which within this shade does dwell:
    To which we nothing Pay or Give,
    They like all other Poets live,
Without reward, or thanks for their obliging parts;
    'Tis well if they become not Prey:
The whistling Winds add their less artful strains,
And a grave Base the murmuring Fountains play;
Nature does all this Harmony bestow,
    But to our Plants, Arts Musick too,
The Pipe, Theorbo, and Guitar we owe;
The Lute it self, which once was Green and Mute,
    When Orpheus strook th' inspired Lute,
    The trees danc'd round, and understood
    By Sympathy the Voice of Wood.

These are the Spels that to kind Sleep invite,
And nothing does within resistance make,
    Which yet we moderately take;
    Who would not choose to be awake,
While he's incompast round with such delight.
To th' Ear, the Nose, the Touch, the Tast, and Sight:
When Venus would her dear Ascanius keep
A Prisoner in the Downy Bands of Sleep,
She Od'rous Herbs and Flowers beneath him spread
    As the most soft and sweetest Bed;
Not her own Lap would more have charm'd his Head
Who, that has Reason, and his Smell,
Would not among Roses and Jasmin dwell,
    Rather then all his spirits choak
With Exhalations of Durt and Smoak.
    And all th'uncleanness which does drown

In Pestilential Clouds a populous Town?
The earth it self breaths better Perfumes here,
Then all the Femal Men or Women there,
Not without cause, about them bear.

When Epicurus to the World had taught,
    That pleasure was the cheifest Good,
(And was perhaps i'th'right, if rightly understood)
    His life he to his Doctrine brought,
And in a Gardens shade that Sovereign Pleasure sought:
Whoever a true Epicure would be,
May there find cheap and virtuous Luxurie.
Vitellius his Table, which did hold
As many Creatures as the Ark of old:
That Fiscal Table, to which every day
All Countrys did a constant Tribute pay,
Could nothing more delicious afford,
    Then Natures Liberalitie,
Helpt with a little Art and Industry,
Allows the meanest Gard'ners board.
The wanton Tast no Fish, or Fowl can choose,
For which the Grape or Melon she would lose,
Though all th' Inhabitants of Sea and Air
Be lifted in the Gluttons bill of Fare;
    Yet still the Fruits of Earth we see
Plac'd the Third Story high in all her Luxury.

On Clarastella walking in her Garden

See how *Flora* smiles to see
This approaching Deitie!
Where each herb looks young and green
In presence of their coming Queen!
Ceres with all her fragrant store,
Could never boast so sweet a flow'r;
While thus in triumph she doth go
The greater Goddess of the two.
Here the Violet bows to greet
Her with homage to her feet;
There the Lilly pales with white
Got by her reflexed light;
Here a Rose in crimson dye
Blushes through her modestie;
There a Pansie hangs his head
'Bout to shrink into his bed,
'Cause so quickly she pass'd by
Not returning suddenly;
Here the Currants red and white
In yon green bush at her sight
Peep through their shady leaves, and cry
Come eat me, as she passes by;
There a bed of Camomile,
When she presseth it doth smell
More fragrant than the perfum'd East,
Or the *Phoenix* spicie nest;
Here the Pinks in rowes do throng
To guard her as she walks along.
There the flexive Turnsole bends
Guided by the rayes she sends
From her bright eyes, as if thence
It suckt life by influence;
Whilst She the prime and chiefest flow'r
In all the Garden by her pow'r
And onely life-inspiring breath
Like the warm Sun redeems from death
Their drooping heads, and bids them live
To tell us She their sweets did give.

The Garden

How vainly men themselves amaze
To win the Palm, the Oke, or Bayes;
And their uncessant Labours see
Crown'd from some single Herb or Tree.
Whose short and narrow verged Shade
Does prudently their Toyles upbraid;
While all Flow'rs and all Trees do ciose
To weave the Garlands of repose.

Fair quiet, have I found thee here,
And Innocence thy Sister dear!
Mistaken long, I sought you then
In busie Companies of Men.
Your sacred Plants, if here below,
Only among the Plants will grow
Society is all but rude,
To this delicious Solitude.

No white nor red was ever seen
So am'rous as this lovely green.
Fond Lovers, cruel as their Flame,
Cut in these Trees their Mistress name.
Little, Alas, they know, or heed,
How far these Beauties Hers exceed!
Fair Trees! where s'eer your barkes I wound,
No name shall but your own be found.

When we have run our Passions heat,
Love hither makes his best retreat.
The *Gods*, that mortal Beauty chase,
Still in a Tree did end their race.
Apollo hunted *Daphne* so,
Only that She might Laurel grow.
And *Pan* did after *Syrinx* speed,
Not as a Nymph, but for a Reed.

What wond'rous Life in this I lead!
Ripe Apples drop about my head;
The Luscious Clusters of the Vine
Upon my Mouth do crush their Wine;
The Nectaren, and curious Peach,
Into my hands themselves do reach;
Stumbling on Melons, as I pass,
Insnar'd with Flow'rs, I fall on Grass.

Mean while the Mind, from pleasure less,
Withdraws into its happiness:
The Mind, that Ocean where each kind
Does streight its own resemblance find;
Yet it creates, transcending these,
Far other Worlds, and other Seas;
Annihilating all that's made
To a green Thought in a green Shade.

Here at the Fountains sliding foot,
Or at some Fruit-trees mossy root,
Casting the Bodies Vest aside,
My Soul into the boughs does glide:
There like a Bird it sits, and sings,
Then whets, and combs its silver Wings;
And, till prepar'd for longer flight,
Waves in its Plumes the various Light.

Such was that happy Garden-state,
While Man there walk'd without a Mate:
After a Place so pure, and sweet,
What other Help could yet be meet!
But 'twas beyond a Mortal's share
To wander solitary there:
Two Paradises 'twere in one
To live in Paradise alone.

How well the skilful Gardner drew
Of flow'rs and herbes this Dial new;
Where from above the milder Sun
Does through a fragrant Zodiack run;
And, as it works, th' industrious Bee
Computes its time as well as we.
How could such sweet and wholsome Hours
Be reckon'd but with herbs and flow'rs!

The Mower against Gardens

Luxurious Man, to bring his Vice in use,
    Did after him the World seduce :
And from the fields the Flow'rs and Plants allure,
    Where Nature was most plain and pure.
He first enclos'd within the Gardens square
    A dead and standing pool of Air :
And a more luscious Earth for them did knead,
    Which stupifi'd them while it fed.
The Pink grew then as double as his Mind;
    The nutriment did change the kind.
With strange perfumes he did the Roses taint.
    And Flow'rs themselves were taught to paint.
The Tulip, white, did for complexion seek;
    And learn'd to interline its cheek :
Its Onion root they then so high did hold,
    That one was for a Meadow sold.
Another World was search'd, through Oceans new,
    To find the *Marvel of Peru*.
And yet these Rarities might be allow'd,
    To Man, that sov'raign thing and proud;
Had he not dealt between the Bark and Tree,
    Forbidden mixtures there to see.
No Plant now knew the Stock from which it came;
    He grafts upon the Wild the Tame :
That the uncertain and adult'rate fruit
    Might put the Palate in dispute.
His green *Seraglio* has its Eunuchs too;
    Lest any Tyrant him out-doe.
And in the Cherry he does Nature vex,
    To procreate without a Sex.
'Tis all enforc'd; the Fountain and the Grot;
    While the sweet Fields do lye forgot :
Where willing Nature does to all dispence
    A wild and fragrant Innocence :
And *Fauns* and *Faryes* do the Meadows till,
    More by their presence then their skill.
Their Statues polish'd by some ancient hand,
    May to adorn the Gardens stand :
But howso'ere the Figures do excel,
    The *Gods* themselves with us do dwell.

I sowed the seeds of love

I sowed the seeds of love
And I sowed them in the spring,
I planted them in my garden fair
While the small birds they did sing.

My garden was well planted
With flowers everywhere,
But I had not the liberty to choose for myself
The flower that I loved so dear.

The gardener standing by
I asked him to choose for me;
He chose me the violet, the lily and the pink,
But these I refused all three.

The violet I did not like
Because it fades so soon;
The lily and the pink I did overthink,
But vowed I would wait till June.

In June is the red, red rose,
And that's the flower for me;
I plucked and I pulled at the red rosy bud
Till I gained the willow tree.

The willow tree will twist,
And the willow tree will twine,
And I wish I were in that young man's arms
That first had this heart of mine.

The Dying Man in his Garden

Why, Damon, with the forward day
Dost thou thy little spot survey,
From tree to tree, with doubtful cheer,
Observe the progress of the year,
What winds arise, what rains descend,
When thou before that year shalt end?

What do thy noonday walks avail,
To clear the leaf, and pick the snail
Then wantonly to death decree
An insect usefuller than thee?
Thou and the worm are brother-kind,
As low, as earthly, and as blind.

Vain wretch! canst thou expect to see
The downy peach make court to thee?
Or that thy sense shall ever meet
The bean-flower's deep-embossom'd sweet
Exhaling with an evening's blast?
Thy evenings then will all be past!

Thy narrow pride, thy fancied green
(For vanity 's in little seen),
All must be left when Death appears
In spite of wishes, groans, and tears
Nor one of all thy plants that grow
But Rosemary will with thee go.

The Butterfly and the Snail

All upstarts, insolent in place,
Remind us of their vulgar race.
  As, in the sun-shine of the morn,
A Butterfly (but newly born)
Sate proudly perking on a rose;
With pert conceit his bosom glows,
His wings (all glorious to behold)
Bedropt with azure, jet and gold,
Wide he displays; the spangled dew
Reflects his eyes and various hue.
  His now forgotten friend, a Snail,
Beneath his house, with slimy trail
Crawles o'er the grass; whom when he spys,
In wrath he to the gard'ner crys:
  What means yon peasant's daily toil,
From choaking weeds to rid the soil?
Why wake you to the morning's care?
Why with new arts correct the year?
Why glows the peach with crimson hue?
And why the plum's inviting blue?
Were they to feast his taste design'd,
That vermine of voracious kind?
Crush then the slow, the pilfring race,
So purge thy garden from disgrace.
  What arrogance! the Snail reply'd;
How insolent is upstart pride!
Hadst thou not thus, with insult vain,
Provok'd my patience to complain;
I had conceal'd thy meaner birth,
Nor trac'd thee to the scum of earth.
For scarce nine suns have wak'd the hours,
To swell the fruit and paint the flowers,
Since I thy humbler life survey'd,
In base, in sordid guise array'd;
A hideous insect, vile, unclean,
You dragg'd a slow and noisome train,
And from your spider bowels drew
Foul film, and spun the dirty clue.
I own my humble life, good friend;
Snail was I born, and snail shall end.
And what's a butterfly? At best,
He's but a caterpillar, drest:
And all thy race (a num'rous seed)
Shall prove of caterpillar breed.

The Gardens of Alcinous
TRANSLATED FROM HOMER'S 'ODYSSEY'

Close to the gates a spacious garden lies,
From storms defended, and inclement skies:
Four acres was th' allotted space of ground,
Fenc'd with a green enclosure all around.
Tall thriving trees confess'd the fruitful mold;
The red'ning apple ripens here to gold,
Here the blue fig with luscious juice o'erflows,
With deeper red the full pomegranate glows,
The branch here bends beneath the weighty pear,
And verdant olives flourish round the year.
The balmy spirit of the western gale
Eternal breathes on fruits untaught to fail:
Each dropping pear a following pear supplies,
On apples apples, figs on figs arise:
The same mild season gives the blooms to blow,
The buds to harden, and the fruits to grow.
    Here order'd vines in equal ranks appear
With all th' united labours of the year,
Some to unload the fertile branches run,
Some dry the black'ning clusters in the sun,
Others to tread the liquid harvest join,
The groaning presses foam with floods of wine.
Here are the vines in early flow'r descry'd,
Here grapes discolour'd on the sunny side.
And there in autumn's richest purple dy'd.
    Beds of all various herbs, for ever green,
In beauteous order terminate the scene.
    Two plenteous fountains the whole
                          prospect crown'd;
This thro' the gardens leads its streams around,
Visits each plant, and waters all the ground:
While that in pipes beneath the palace flows,
And thence its current on the town bestows;
To various use their various streams they bring,
The People one, and one supplies the King.

Spring Flowers

Along the blushing borders bright with dew,
And in yon mingled wilderness of flowers,
Fair-handed Spring unbosoms every grace :
Throws out the snow-drop and the crocus first ;
The daisy, primrose, violet darkly blue,
And polyanthus of unnumbered dyes ;
The yellow wall-flower, stained with iron brown,
And lavish stock that scents the garden round :
From the soft wing of vernal breezes shed,
Anemonies ; auriculas, enriched
With shining meal o'er all their velvet leaves ;
And full ranunculas, of glowing red.
Then comes the tulip-race, where Beauty plays
Her idle freaks : from family diffused
To family, as flies the father-dust,
The varied colours run ; and while they break
On the charmed eye, the exulting florist marks,
With secret pride, the wonders of his hand.
No gradual bloom is wanting ; from the bud,
First-born of Spring, to Summer's musky tribes :
Nor hyacinths, deep-purpled ; nor jonquils,
Of potent fragrance ; nor narcissus fair,
As o'er the fabled fountain hanging still ;
Nor broad carnations, nor gay-spotted pinks ;
Nor, showered from every bush, the damask-rose :
Infinite numbers, delicacies, smells,
With hues on hues expression cannot paint,
The breath of Nature, and her endless bloom.

To a worm which the author accidentally trode upon

Methinks thou writhest as in rage;—
  But, dying reptile, know,
Thou ow'st to chance thy death!—I scorn
  To crush my meanest foe.

Anger, 'tis true, and justice stern
  Might fairly here have place.—
Are not thy subterraneous tribes
  Devourers of our race?

On princes they have richly fed,
  When their vast work was done;
And monarchs have regal'd vile worms,
  Who first the world had won.

Let vengeance then thine exit cheer,
  Nor at thy fate repine:
Legions of worms (who knows how soon?)
  Shall feast on me, and mine.

The Charms of Nature
FROM 'THE ENTHUSIAST', OR THE LOVER OF NATURE

Rich in her weeping country's spoils, Versailles
May boast a thousand fountains, that can cast
The tortur'd waters to the distant heav'ns;
Yet let me choose some pine-top'd precipice
Abrupt and shaggy, whence a foamy stream,
Like Anio, tumbling roars; or some bleak heath,
Where straggling stand the mournful juniper,
Or yew-tree scath'd; while in clear prospect round,
From the grove's bosom spires emerge, and smoak
In bluish wreaths ascends, ripe harvests wave,
Low, lonely cottages, and ruin'd tops
Of Gothick battlements appear, and streams
Beneath the sun-beams twinkle. The shrill lark,
That wakes the wood-man to his early task,
Or love-sick Philomel, whose luscious lays
Sooth lone night-wanderers, the moaning dove
Pitied by listening milk-maid, far excell
The deep-mouth'd viol, the soul-lulling lute,
And battle-breathing trumpet. Artful sounds!
That please not like the choristers of air,
When first they hail th' approach of laughing May.

O taste corrupt! that luxury and pomp,
In specious names of polish'd manners veil'd,
Should proudly banish Nature's simple charms!
All-beauteous Nature! by thy boundless charms
Oppress'd, O where shall I begin thy praise,
Where turn th' ecstatick eye, how ease my breast
That pants with wild astonishment and love!
Dark forests, and the opening lawn, refresh'd
With ever-gushing brooks, hill, meadow, dale,
The balmy bean-field, the gay-clover'd close,
So sweetly interchang'd, the lowing ox,
The playful lamb, the distant water-fall
Now faintly heard, now swelling with the breeze,
The sound of pastoral reed from hazel-bower,
The choral birds, the neighing steed, that snuffs
His dappled mate, stung with intense desire,
The ripen'd orchard when the ruddy orbs
Betwixt the green leaves blush, the azure skies,
The chearful sun that thro' earth's vitals pours
Delight and health and heat; all, all conspire

To raise, to sooth, to harmonize the mind,
To lift on wings of praise, to the great sire
Of being and of beauty, at whose nod
Creation started from the gloomy vault
Of dreary Chaos, while the griesly king
Murmur'd to feel his boisterous power confin'd.
What are the lays of artful Addison,
Coldly correct, to Shakespeare's warblings wild?
Whom on the winding Avon's willow'd banks
Fair fancy found, and bore the smiling babe
To a close cavern: (still the shepherds shew
The sacred place, whence with religious awe
They hear, returning from the field at eve,
Strange whisp'ring of sweet musick thro' the air)
Here, as with honey gather'd from the rock,
She fed the little prattler, and with songs
Oft' sooth'd his wondering ears, with deep delight
On her soft lap he sat, and caught the sounds.

Garden Plants
FROM 'THE ENGLISH GARDEN'

Nor are the plants which England calls her own
Few or unlovely, that, with laurel join'd
And kindred foliage of perennial green,
Will form a close-knit curtain. Shrubs there are
Of bolder growth, that, at the call of Spring,
Burst forth in blossom'd fragrance: lilacs rob'd
In snow-white innocence, or purple pride;
The sweet syringa yielding but in scent
To the rich orange; or the woodbine wild
That loves to hang, on barren boughs remote,
Her wreaths of flowery perfume. These beside,
Myriads, that here the Muse neglects to name,
Will add a vernal lustre to thy veil.

   And what if chance collects the varied tribes,
Yet fear not thou but unexpected charms
Will from their union start. But if our song
Supply one precept here, it bids retire
Each leaf of deeper dye, and lift in front
Foliage of paler verdure, so to spread
A canvass, which when touch'd by Autumn's hand
Shall gleam with dusky gold, or russet rays.
But why prepare for her funereal hand
That canvass? she but comes to dress thy shades,
As lovelier victims for their wintry tomb.
Rather to flowery Spring, to Summer bright,
Thy labour consecrate; their laughing reign,
The youth, the manhood of the growing year,
Deserves that labour, and rewards its pain.
Yet, heedful ever of that ruthless time
When Winter shakes their stems, preserve a file
With everduring leaf to brave his arm,
And deepening spread their undiminish'd gloom.

The Village
FROM 'THE DESERTED VILLAGE'

Sweet smiling village, loveliest of the lawn,
Thy sports are fled, and all thy charms withdrawn;
Amidst thy bowers the tyrant's hand is seen,
And desolation saddens all thy green:
One only master grasps the whole domain,
And half a tillage stints thy smiling plain;
No more thy glassy brook reflects the day,
But choaked with sedges, works its weedy way.
Along thy glades, a solitary guest,
The hollow sounding bittern guards its nest;

Amidst thy desert walks the lapwing flies,
And tires their ecchoes with unvaried cries.
Sunk are thy bowers in shapeless ruin all,
And the long grass o'ertops the mouldering wall,
And trembling, shrinking from the spoiler's hand,
Far, far away thy children leave the land.

Ill fares the land, to hastening ills a prey,
Where wealth accumulates, and men decay;
Princes and lords may flourish, or may fade;
A breath can make them, as a breath has made.
But a bold peasantry, their country's pride,
When once destroyed, can never be supplied.

A time there was, ere England's griefs began,
When every rood of ground maintained its man;
For him light labour spread her wholesome store,
Just gave what life required, but gave no more.
His best companions, innocence and health;
And his best riches, ignorance of wealth.

The Shrubbery

WRITTEN IN A TIME OF AFFLICTION

Oh, happy shades—to me unblest,
    Friendly to peace, but not to me,
How ill the scene that offers rest,
    And heart that cannot rest, agree!

This glassy stream, that spreading pine,
    Those alders quivering to the breeze,
Might sooth a soul less hurt than mine,
    And please, if any thing could please.

But fixed unalterable care
    Foregoes not what she feels within,
Shows the same sadness everywhere,
    And slights the season and the scene.

For all that pleased in wood or lawn,
    While peace possessed these silent bowers,
Her animating smile withdrawn,
    Has lost its beauties and its powers.

The saint or moralist should tread
    This moss-grown alley, musing, slow;
They seek, like me, the secret shade,
    But not, like me, to nourish woe.

Me fruitful scenes and prospects waste
    Alike admonish not to roam;
These tell me of enjoyments past,
    And those of sorrows yet to come.

Capability Brown
FROM 'THE TASK'

Improvement too, the idol of the age,
Is fed with many a victim. Lo, he comes!
Th' omnipotent magician, Brown, appears!
Down falls the venerable pile, th' abode
Of our forefathers—a grave whisker'd race,
But tasteless. Springs a palace in its stead,
But in a distant spot; where, more expos'd,
It may enjoy th' advantage of the north,
And aguish east, till time shall have transform'd
Those naked acres to a shelt'ring grove.
He speaks. The lake in front becomes a lawn;
Woods vanish, hills subside, and valleys rise:
And streams, as if created for his use,
Pursue the track of his directing wand,
Sinuous or straight, now rapid and now slow,
Now murm'ring soft, now roaring in cascades—
Ev'n as he bids! Th' enraptur'd owner smiles.
'Tis finish'd, and yet, finish'd as it seems,
Still wants a grace, the loveliest it could show,
A mine to satisfy th' enormous cost.
Drain'd to the last poor item of his wealth,
He sighs, departs, and leaves th' accomplish'd plan
That he has touch'd, retouch'd, many a long day
Labour'd, and many a night pursu'd in dreams,
Just when it meets his hopes, and proves the heav'n
He wanted, for a wealthier to enjoy!

Song

How sweet I roam'd from field to field
And tasted all the summer's pride,
Till I the prince of love beheld
Who in the sunny beams did glide!

He shew'd me lilies for my hair,
And blushing roses for my brow;
He led me through his gardens fair
Where all his golden pleasures grow.

With sweet May dews my wings were wet,
And Phoebus fir'd my vocal rage;
He caught me in his silken net,
And shut me in his golden cage.

He loves to sit and hear me sing,
Then, laughing, sports and plays with me;
Then stretches out my golden wing,
And mocks my loss of liberty.

The Garden of Love
FROM 'SONGS OF EXPERIENCE'

I went to the Garden of Love,
And saw what I never had seen:
A Chapel was built in the midst,
Where I used to play on the green.

And the gates of this Chapel were shut,
And 'Thou shalt not' writ over the door;
So I turn'd to the Garden of Love
That so many sweet flowers bore;

And I saw it was filled with graves,
And tomb-stones where flowers should be;
And Priests in black gowns were walking their rounds,
And binding with briars my joys and desires.

When rosy May comes in wi' flowers

When rosy May comes in wi' flowers
To deck her gay, green-spreading bowers,
Then busy, busy are his hours
   The gard'ner wi' his paidle.

The crystal waters gently fa'
The merry birds are lovers a'
The scented breezes round him blaw,
   The gard'ner wi' his paidle.

When purple morning starts the hare
To steal upon her early fare,
Then thro' the dew he maun repair—
   The gard'ner wi' his paidle.

When day, expiring in the West,
The curtain draws o' Nature's rest,
He flies to her arms he lo'es best,
   The gard'ner wi' his paidle.

The Groves of Blarney

The groves of Blarney
They look so charming,
Down by the purling
   Of sweet, silent brooks,
Being banked with posies
That spontaneous grow there,
Planted in order
   By the sweet 'Rock Close'.
'Tis there the daisy
And the sweet carnation,
The blooming pink
   And the rose so fair,
The daffydowndilly,
Likewise the lily,
All flowers that scent
   The sweet, fragrant air.

'Tis Lady Jeffers
That owns this station;
Like Alexander
   Or Queen Helen fair
There's no commander
In all the nation,
For emulation,
   Can with her compare.
Such walls surround her,
That no nine-pounder
Could dare to plunder
   Her place of strength;
But Oliver Cromwell
Her he did pommell,
And made a breach
   In her battlement.

There's gravel walks there
For speculation
And conversation
   In sweet solitude.
'Tis there the lover
May hear the dove, or
The gentle plover
   In the afternoon;

And if a lady
Would be so engaging
As to walk alone in
   Those shady bowers,
'Tis there the courtier
He may transport her
Into some fort, or
   All underground.

For 'tis there's a cave where
No daylight enters,
But cats and badgers
   Are for ever bred;
Being mossed by nature,
That makes it sweeter
Than a coach-and six or
   A feather bed.
'Tis there the lake is,
Well stored with perches,
And comely eels in
   The verdant mud;
Besides the leeches,
And groves of beeches,
Standing in order
   For to guard the flood.

There's statues gracing
This noble place in—
All heathen gods
   And nymphs so fair;
Bold Neptune, Plutarch,
And Nicodemus,
All standing naked
   In the open air!
So now to finish
This brave narration,
Which my poor genii
   Could not entwine;
But were I Homer,
Or Nebuchadnezzar,
'Tis in every feature
   I would make it shine.

A Farewell

Farewell, thou little Nook of mountain-ground,
Thou rocky corner in the lowest stair
Of that magnificent temple which doth bound
One side of our whole vale with grandeur rare;
Sweet garden-orchard, eminently fair,
The loveliest spot that man hath ever found,
Farewell!—we leave thee to Heaven's peaceful care,
Thee, and the Cottage which thou dost surround.

Our boat is safely anchored by the shore,
And there will safely ride when we are gone;
The flowering shrubs that deck our humble door
Will prosper, though untended and alone:
Fields, goods, and far-off chattels we have none:
These narrow bounds contain our private store
Of things earth makes, and sun doth shine upon:
Here are they in our sight—we have no more.

Sunshine and shower be with you, bud and bell!
For two months now in vain we shall be sought;
We leave you here in solitude to dwell
With these our latest gifts of tender thought;
Thou, like the morning, in thy saffron coat,
Bright gowan, and marsh-marigold, farewell!
Whom from the borders of the Lake we brought,
And placed together near our rocky Well.

We go for One to whom ye will be dear;
And she will prize this Bower, this Indian shed,
Our own contrivance, Building without peer!
—A gentle Maid, whose heart is lowly bred,
Whose pleasures are in wild fields gatherèd,
With joyousness, and with a thoughtful cheer,
Will come to you; to you herself will wed;
And love the blessed life that we lead here.

Dear Spot! which we have watched with tender heed,
Bringing thee chosen plants and blossoms blown
Among the distant mountains, flower and weed,
Which thou hast taken to thee as thy own,
Making all kindness registered and known;
Thou for our sakes, though Nature's child indeed,
Fair in thyself and beautiful alone,
Hast taken gifts which thou dost little need.

And O most constant, yet most fickle Place,
That hast thy wayward moods, as thou dost show
To them who look not daily on thy face;
Who, being loved, in love no bounds dost know,
And say'st, when we forsake thee, 'Let them go!'
Thou easy-hearted Thing, with thy wild race
Of weeds and flowers, till we return be slow,
And travel with the year at a soft pace.

Help us to tell Her tales of years gone by,
And this sweet spring, the best beloved and best;
Joy will be flown in its mortality;
Something must stay to tell us of the rest.
Here, thronged with primroses, the steep rock's breast
Glittered at evening like a starry sky;
And in this bush our sparrow built her nest,
Of which I sang one song that will not die.

O happy Garden! whose seclusion deep
Hath been so friendly to industrious hours;
And to soft slumbers, that did gently steep
Our spirits, carrying with them dreams of flowers,
And wild notes warbled among leafy bowers;
Two burning months let summer overleap,
And, coming back with Her who will be ours,
Into thy bosom we again shall creep.

In a Garden in the Grounds of Coleorton, Leicestershire

Oft is the medal faithful to its trust
When temples, columns, towers, are laid in dust;
And 'tis a common ordinance of fate
That things obscure and small outlive the great:
Hence, when yon mansion and the flowery trim
Of this fair garden, and its alleys dim,
And all its stately trees, are passed away,
This little Niche, unconscious of decay,
Perchance may still survive. And be it known
That it was scooped within the living stone,—
Not by the sluggish and ungrateful pains
Of labourer plodding for his daily gains,
But by an industry that wrought in love;
With help from female hands, that proudly strove
To aid the work, what time these walks and bowers
Were shaped to cheer dark winter's lonely hours.

Reflections on having left a
Place of Retirement

Low was our pretty Cot: our tallest Rose
Peep'd at the chamber-window. We could hear
At silent noon, and eve, and early morn,
The Sea's faint murmur. In the open air
Our Myrtles blossom'd; and across the porch
Thick Jasmins twined: the little landscape round
Was green and woody, and refresh'd the eye.
It was a spot which you might aptly call
The Valley of Seclusion! Once I saw
(Hallowing his Sabbath-day by quietness)
A wealthy son of Commerce saunter by,
Bristowa's citizen: methought, it calm'd
His thirst of idle gold, and made him muse
With wiser feelings: for he paus'd, and look'd
With a pleas'd sadness, and gaz'd all around,
Then eyed our Cottage, and gaz'd round again,
And sigh'd, and said, it was a Blesséd Place.
And we *were* bless'd. Oft with patient ear
Long-listening to the viewless sky-lark's note
(Viewless, or haply for a moment seen
Gleaming on sunny wings) in whisper'd tones
I've said to my belovéd, 'Such, sweet Girl!
The inobtrusive song of Happiness,
Unearthly minstrelsy! then only heard
When the Soul seeks to hear; when all is hush'd,
And the Heart listens!'
                              But the time, when first
From that low Dell, steep up the stony Mount
I climb'd with perilous toil and reach'd the top,
Oh! what a goodly scene! *Here* the bleak mount,
The bare bleak mountain speckled thin with sheep;
Grey clouds, that shadowing spot the sunny fields;
And river, now with bushy rocks o'er-brow'd,
Now winding bright and full, with naked banks;
And seats, and lawns, the Abbey and the wood,
And cots, and hamlets, and faint city-spire;
The Channel *there*, the Islands and white sails,
Dim coasts, and cloud-like hills, and
                                         shoreless Ocean—
It seem'd like Omnipresence! God, methought,
Had built him there a Temple: the whole World
Seem'd *imag'd* in its vast circumference:
No *wish* profan'd my overwhelméd heart.
Blest hour! It was a luxury,—to be!

Ah! quiet Dell! dear Cot, and Mount sublime!
I was constrain'd to quit you. Was it right,
While my unnumber'd brethren toil'd and bled,
That I should dream away the entrusted hours
On rose-leaf beds, pampering the coward heart
With feelings all too delicate for use?
Sweet is the tear that from some Howard's eye
Drops on the cheek of one he lifts from earth:
And he that works me good with unmov'd face,
Does it but half: he chills me while he aids,
My benefactor, not my brother man!
Yet even this, this cold beneficence
Praise, praise it, O my Soul! oft as thou scann'st
The sluggard Pity's vision-weaving tribe!
Who sigh for Wretchedness, yet shun the Wretched,
Nursing in some delicious solitude
Their slothful loves and dainty sympathies!
I therefore go, and join head, heart, and hand,
Active and firm, to fight the bloodless fight
Of Science, Freedom, and the Truth in Christ.

Yet oft when after honourable toil
Rests the tir'd mind, and waking loves to dream,
My spirit shall revisit thee, dear Cot!
Thy Jasmin and thy window-peeping Rose,
And Myrtles fearless of the mild sea-air.
And I shall sigh fond wishes—sweet Abode!
Ah!—had none greater! And that all had such!
It might be so—but the time is not yet.
Speed it, O Father! Let thy Kingdom come!

A House and Grounds

Were this impossible, I know full well
What sort of house should grace my garden-bell,—
A good, old country lodge, half hid with blooms
Of honied green, and quaint with straggling rooms,
A few of which, white-bedded and well swept,
For friends, whose names endear'd them,
                                        should be kept.
Of brick I'd have it, far more broad than high,
With green up to the door, and elm trees nigh;
And the warm sun should have it in his eye.
The tiptoe traveller, peeping through the boughs
O'er my low wall, should bless the pleasant house,
And that my luck might not seem ill-bestow'd,
A bench and spring should greet him on the road.
My grounds should not be large; I like to go
To Nature for a range, and prospect too,
And cannot fancy she'll comprise for me,
Even in a park, her all-sufficiency.
Besides, my thoughts fly far; and when at rest,
Love, not a watch tower, but a lulling nest.
But all the ground I had should keep a look
Of Nature still, have birds'-nests and a brook;
One spot for flowers, the rest all turf and trees;
For I'd not grow my own bad lettuces.
I'd build a walk, however, against rain,
Long, peradventure, as my whole domain,
And so be sure of generous exercise,
The youth of age, and med'cine of the wise.
And this reminds me, that behind some screen
About my grounds, I'd have a bowling-green;
Such as in wits' and merry women's days
Suckling preferred before his walk of bays.
You may still see them, dead as haunts of fairies,
By the old seats of Killigrews and Careys,
Where all, alas, is vanished from the ring,
Wits and black eyes, the skittles and the king!

Merlin's Apple-trees
FROM 'MISFORTUNES OF ELPHIN'

Fair the gift to Merlin given,
Apple-trees seven score and seven
Equal all in age and size;
On a green hill-slope, that lies
Basking in the southern sun,
Where bright waters murmuring run.

Just beneath the pure stream flows;
High above the forest grows;
Not again on earth is found
Such a slope of orchard ground:
Song of birds, and hum of bees,
Ever haunt the apple-trees.

Lovely green their leaves in spring;
Lovely bright their blossoming:
Sweet the shelter and the shade
By their summer foliage made:
Sweet the fruit their ripe boughs hold,
Fruit delicious, tinged with gold.

Gloyad, nymph with tresses bright,
Teeth of pearl, and eyes of light,
Guards these gifts of Ceidio's son,
Gwendol, the lamented one,
Him, whose keen-edged sword no more
Flashes 'mid the battle's roar.

War has raged on vale and hill:
That fair grove was peaceful still.
There have chiefs and princes sought
Solitude and tranquil thought:
There have kings, from courts and throngs,
Turned to Merlin's wild-wood songs.

Now from echoing woods I hear
Hostile axes sounding near:
On the sunny slope reclined,
Feverish grief disturbs my mind,
Lest the wasting edge consume
My fair spot of fruit and bloom.

Lovely trees, that long alone
In the sylvan vale have grown,
Bare, your sacred plot around,
Grows the once wood-waving ground:
Fervent valour guards ye still;
Yet my soul presages ill.

Well I know, when years have flown,
Briars shall grow where ye have grown:
Them in turn shall power uproot;
Then again shall flowers and fruit
Flourish in the sunny breeze,
On my new-born apple-trees.

GEORGE GORDON, LORD BYRON   1788–1824

Love's Last Adieu
'Αεὶ δ' ἀεί με φεύγει ANACREON

The roses of love glad the garden of life,
Though nurtured 'mid weeds dropping pestilent dew,
Till time crops the leaves with unmerciful knife,
Or prunes them for ever, in love's last adieu!

In vain with endearments we soothe the sad heart,
In vain do we vow for an age to be true;
The chance of an hour may command us to part,
Or death disunite us in love's last adieu!

Still Hope, breathing peace through the
                                    grief-swollen breast,
Will whisper, 'Our meeting we yet may renew':
With this dream of deceit half our sorrow's represt,
Nor taste we the poison of love's last adieu!

Oh! mark you yon pair: in the sunshine of youth
Love twined round their childhood his flow'rs
                                          as they grew;
They flourish awhile in the season of truth,
Till chill'd by the winter of love's last adieu!

Sweet lady! why thus doth a tear steal its way
Down a cheek which outrivals thy bosom in hue?
Yet why do I ask?—to distraction a prey,
Thy reason has perish'd with love's last adieu!

Oh! who is yon misanthrope, shunning mankind?
From cities to caves of the forest he flew
There, raving, he howls his complaint to the wind;
The mountains reverberate love's last adieu!

Now hate rules a heart which in love's easy chains
Once passion's tumultuous blandishments knew;
Despair now inflames the dark tide of his veins;
He ponders in frenzy on love's last adieu!

How he envies the wretch with a soul wrapt in steel!
His pleasures are scarce, yet his troubles are few,
Who laughs at the pang that he never can feel,
And dreads not the anguish of love's last adieu!

Youth flies, life decays, even hope is o'ercast:
No more with love's former devotion we sue:
He spreads his young wing, he retires with the blast;
The shroud of affection is love's last adieu!

In this life of probation for rapture divine,
Astrea declares that some penance is due;
From him who has worshipp'd at love's gentle shrine,
The atonement is ample in love's last adieu!

Who kneels to the god, on his altar of light
Must myrtle and cypress alternately strew:
His myrtle, an emblem of purest delight;
His cypress the garland of love's last adieu!

The Garden
FROM 'THE SENSITIVE PLANT'

There was a Power in this sweet place,
An Eve in this Eden; a ruling Grace
Which to the flowers, did they waken or dream,
Was as God is to the starry scheme.

A Lady, the wonder of her kind,
Whose form was upborne by a lovely mind
Which, dilating, had molded her mien and motion
Like a sea-flower unfolded beneath the ocean,

Tended the garden from morn to even:
And the meteors of that sublunar Heaven,
Like the lamps of the air when Night walks forth,
Laughed round her footsteps up from the Earth!

She had no companion of mortal race,
But her tremulous breath and her flushing face
Told, whilst the morn kissed the sleep from her eyes,
That her dreams were less slumber than Paradise:

As if some bright Spirit for her sweet sake
Had deserted Heaven while the stars were awake,
As if yet around her he lingering were,
Though the veil of daylight concealed him from her.

Her step seemed to pity the grass it pressed;
You might hear by the heaving of her breast,
That the coming and going of the wind
Brought pleasure there and left passion behind.

And wherever her aëry footstep trod,
Her trailing hair from the grassy sod
Erased its light vestige, with shadowy sweep,
Like a sunny storm o'er the dark green deep.

I doubt not the flowers of that garden sweet
Rejoiced in the sound of her gentle feet;
I doubt not they felt the spirit that came
From her glowing fingers through all their frame.

She sprinkled bright water from the stream
On those that were faint with the sunny beam;
And out of the cups of the heavy flowers
She emptied the rain of the thunder-showers.

She lifted their heads with her tender hands,
And sustained them with rods and osier-bands;
If the flowers had been her own infants, she
Could never have nursed them more tenderly.

And all killing insects and gnawing worms,
And things of obscene and unlovely forms,
She bore, in a basket of Indian woof,
Into the rough woods far aloof—

In a basket, of grasses and wild-flowers full,
The freshest her gentle hands could pull
For the poor banished insects, whose intent,
Although they did ill, was innocent.

But the bee and the beamlike ephemeris
Whose path is the lightning's, and soft moths that kiss
The sweet lips of the flowers, and harm not, did she
Make her attendant angels be.

And many an antenatal tomb,
Where butterflies dream of the life to come,
She left clinging round the smooth and dark
Edge of the odorous cedar bark.

This fairest creature from earliest Spring
Thus moved through the garden ministering
All the sweet season of Summertide,
And ere the first leaf looked brown—she died!

Proposals for Building a Cottage

Beside a runnel build my shed,
With stubbles cover'd o'er;
Let broad oaks o'er its chimney spread,
    And grass-plats grace the door.

The door may open with a string,
    So that it closes tight;
And locks would be a wanted thing,
    To keep out thieves at night.

A little garden, not too fine,
    Inclose with painted pales;
And woodbines, round the cot to twine,
    Pin to the wall with nails.

Let hazels grow, and spindling sedge,
    Bend bowering over-head;
Dig old man's beard from woodland hedge,
    To twine a summer shade.

Beside the threshold sods provide,
    And build a summer seat;
Plant sweet-briar bushes by its side,
    And flowers that blossom sweet.

I love the sparrow's ways to watch
    Upon the cotter's sheds,
So here and there pull out the thatch,
    That they may hide their heads.

And as the sweeping swallows stop
    Their flights along the green,
Leave holes within the chimney-top
    To paste their nest between.

Stick shelves and cupboards round the hut,
    In all the holes and nooks;
Nor in the corner fail to put
    A cupboard for the books.

Along the floor some sand I'll sift,
    To make it fit to live in;
And then I'll thank ye for the gift,
    As something worth the giving.

To Autumn

Season of mists and mellow fruitfulness!
  Close bosom-friend of the maturing sun;
Conspiring with him how to load and bless
  With fruit the vines that round the thatch-eaves run;
To bend with apples the mossed cottage-trees,
  And fill all fruit with ripeness to the core;
    To swell the gourd, and plump the hazel shells
With a sweet kernel; to set budding more,
  And still more, later flowers for the bees,
  Until they think warm days will never cease,
    For Summer has o'erbrimmed their clammy cells.

Who hath not seen thee oft amid thy store?
  Sometimes whoever seeks abroad may find
Thee sitting careless on a granary floor,
  Thy hair soft-lifted by the winnowing wind,
Or on a half-reaped furrow sound asleep,
  Drowsed with the fume of poppies, while thy hook
    Spares the next swath and all its twinèd flowers;
And sometimes like a gleaner thou dost keep
  Steady thy laden head across a brook;
  Or by a cider-press, with patient look,
    Thou watchest the last oozings hours by hours.

Where are the songs of Spring? Ay, where are they?
  Think not of them, thou hast thy music too,—
While barred clouds bloom the soft-dying day,
  And touch the stubble-plains with rosy hue;
Then in a wailful choir the small gnats mourn
  Among the river sallows, borne aloft
    Or sinking as the light wind lives or dies;
And full-grown lambs loud bleat from hilly bourn;
  Hedge-crickets sing; and now with treble soft
  The redbreast whistles from a garden-croft;
    And gathering swallows twitter in the skies.

I remember, I remember

air must rush as fresh
                          I remember, I remember
The house where I was born,
The little window where the sun
Came peeping in at morn ;
He never came a wink too soon
Nor brought too long a day ;
But now, I often wish the night
Had borne my breath away.

I remember, I remember
The roses, red and white,
The violets, and the lily-cups—
Those flowers made of light !
The lilacs where the robin built,
And where my brother set
The laburnum on his birthday,—
The tree is living yet !

I remember, I remember
Where I used to swing,
And thought the air must rush as fresh
To swallows on the wing ;
My spirit flew in feathers then
That is so heavy now,
And summer pools could hardly cool
The fever on my brow.

I remember, I remember
The fir trees dark and high ;
I used to think their slender tops
Were close against the sky :
It was a childish ignorance,
But now 'tis little joy
To know I'm farther off from heaven
Than when I was a boy.

The Hwomestead

If I had all the land my zight
  Can overlook vrom Chalwell hill,
Vrom Sherborn left to Blanvord right,
  Why I could be but happy still.
An' I be happy wi' my spot
O' freehold ground an' mossy cot,
An' shoulden get a better lot
  If I had all my will.

My orcha'd's wide, my trees be young;
  An' they do bear such heavy crops,
Their boughs, lik' onion rwopes a-hung,
  Be all a-trigg'd to-year, wi' props.
I got some geärden groun' to dig,
A parrock, an' a cow an' pig;
I got zome cider vor to swig,
  An' eäle o' malt an' hops.

I'm landlord o' my little farm,
  I'm king 'ithin my little pleäce;
I don't break laws, an' don't do harm,
  An' ben't afeärd o' noo man's feäce.
When I'm a-cover'd wi' my thatch,
Noo man do deäre to lift my latch;
Where honest han's do shut the hatch,
  There fear do leäve the pleäce.

My lofty elem trees do screen
  My brown-ruf'd house, an' here below,
My geese do strut athirt the green,
  An' hiss an' flap their wings o' snow;
As I do walk along a rank
Ov apple trees, or by a bank,
Or zit upon a bar or plank,
  To zee how things do grow.

Beloved, thou has brought me many flowers

SONNET XLIV, FROM THE PORTUGUESE

Belovèd, thou has brought me many flowers
Plucked in the garden, all the summer through
And winter, and it seemed as if they grew
In this close room, nor missed the sun and showers.
So, in the like name of that love of ours,
Take back these thoughts which here unfolded too,
And which on warm and cold days I withdrew
From my heart's ground. Indeed, those beds and bowers
Be overgrown with bitter weeds and rue,
And wait thy weeding; yet here's eglantine,
Here's ivy!—take them, as I used to do
Thy flowers, and keep them where they shall not pine.
Instruct thine eyes to keep their colours true,
And tell thy soul their roots are left in mine.

CHARLES TENNYSON TURNER   1808—79

A Summer Twilight

as the snow-flake, leaves his lair;
                              It is a Summer gloaming,
balmy-sweet,
A gloaming brighten'd by an infant moon,
Fraught with the fairest light of middle June;
The lonely garden echoes to my feet,
And hark! O hear I not the gentle dews,
Fretting the silent forest in his sleep?
Or does the stir of housing insects creep
Thus faintly on mine ear? Day's many hues
Waned with the paling light and are no more,
And none but drowsy pinions beat the air:
The bat is hunting softly by my door,
And, noiseless as the snow-flake, leaves his lair;
O'er the still copses flitting here and there,
Wheeling the self-same circuit o'er and o'er.

I sometimes think that never blows so red
FROM 'THE RUBAIYAT OF OMAR KHAYYAM'

I sometimes think that never blows so red
The rose as where some buried Caesar bled;
    That every hyacinth the garden wears
Dropped in her lap from some once lovely head.

And this reviving herb whose tender green
Fledges the river-lip on which we lean—
    Ah, lean upon it lightly! for who knows
From what once lovely lip it springs unseen!

Come into the garden, Maud
FROM 'MAUD'

Come into the garden, Maud,
    For the black bat, night, has flown,
Come into the garden, Maud,
    I am here at the gate alone;
And the woodbine spices are wafted abroad,
    And the musk of the rose is blown.

For a breeze of morning moves,
    And the planet of Love is on high,
Beginning to faint in the light that she loves
    On a bed of daffodil sky,
To faint in the light of the sun she loves,
    To faint in his light, and to die.

All night have the roses heard
    The flute, violin, bassoon;
All night has the casement jessamine stirr'd
    To the dancers dancing in tune;
Till a silence fell with the waking bird,
    And a hush with the setting moon.

I said to the lily, 'There is but one
　With whom she has heart to be gay.
When will the dancers leave her alone?
　She is weary of dance and play.'
Now half to the setting moon are gone,
　And half to the rising day;
Low on the sand and loud on the stone
　The last wheel echoes away.

I said to the rose, 'The brief night goes
　In babble and revel and wine.
O young lord-lover, what sighs are those,
　For one that will never be thine?
But mine, but mine,' so I sware to the rose,
　'For ever and ever, mine.'

And the soul of the rose went into my blood,
　As the music clash'd in the hall:
And long by the garden lake I stood,
　For I heard your rivulet fall
From the lake to the meadow and on to the wood,
　Our wood, that is dearer than all;

From the meadow your walks have left so sweet
　That whenever a March-wind sighs
He sets the jewel-print of your feet
　In violets blue as your eyes,
To the woody hollows in which we meet
　And the valleys of Paradise.

The slender acacia would not shake
　One long milk-bloom on the tree;
The white lake-blossom fell into the lake
　As the pimpernel dozed on the lea;
But the rose was awake all night for your sake,
　Knowing your promise to me;
The lilies and roses were all awake,
　They sigh'd for the dawn and thee.

Queen rose of the rosebud garden of girls,
　Come hither, the dances are done.
In gloss of satin and glimmer of pearls,
　Queen lily and rose in one;
Shine out, little head, sunning over with curls,
　To the flowers, and be their sun.

There has fallen a splendid tear
   From the passion-flower at the gate.
She is coming, my dove, my dear;
   She is coming, my life, my fate;
The red rose cries, 'She is near, she is near;'
   And the white rose weeps, 'She is late;'
The larkspur listens, 'I hear, I hear;'
   And the lily whispers, 'I wait.'

She is coming, my own, my sweet;
   Were it ever so airy a tread,
My heart would hear her and beat,
   Were it earth in an earthy bed;
My dust would hear her and beat,
   Had I lain for a century dead;
Would start and tremble under her feet,
   And blossom in purple and red.

The Flower

Once in a golden hour
  I cast to earth a seed.
Up there came a flower,
  The people said, a weed.

To and fro they went
  Thro' my garden-bower,
And muttering discontent
  Cursed me and my flower.

Then it grew so tall
  It wore a crown of light,
But thieves from o'er the wall
  Stole the seed by night.

Sow'd it far and wide
  By every town and tower,
Till all the people cried
  'Splendid is the flower.'

Read my little fable:
  He that runs may read.
Most can raise the flowers now,
  For all have got the seed.

And some are pretty enough,
  And some are poor indeed;
And now again the people
  Call it but a weed.

The Flower's Name
FROM 'GARDEN FANCIES'

Here's the garden she walked across,
   Arm in my arm, such a short while since:
Hark, now I push its wicket, the moss
   Hinders the hinges and makes them wince!
She must have reached this shrub ere she turned,
   As back with that murmur the wicket swung;
For she laid the poor snail, my chance foot spurned,
   To feed and forget it the leaves among.

Down this side of the gravel-walk
   She went while her robe's edge brushed the box:
And here she paused in her gracious talk
   To point me a moth on the milk-white phlox.
Roses, ranged in valiant row,
   I will never think that she passed you by!
She loves you noble roses, I know;
   But yonder, see, where the rock-plants lie!

This flower she stopped at, finger on lip,
   Stooped over, in doubt, as settling its claim;
Till she gave me, with pride to make no slip,
   Its soft meandering Spanish name:
What a name! Was it love or praise?
   Speech half-asleep or song half-awake?
I must learn Spanish, one of these days,
   Only for that slow sweet name's sake.

Roses, if I live and do well,
   I may bring her, one of these days,
To fix you fast with as fine a spell,
   Fit you each with his Spanish phrase;
But do not detain me now; for she lingers
   There, like sunshine over the ground,
And ever I see her soft white fingers
   Searching after the bud she found.

Flower, you Spaniard, look that you grow not,
    Stay as you are and be loved for ever!
Bud, if I kiss you 'tis that you blow not:
    Mind, the shut pink mouth opens never!
For while it pouts, her fingers wrestle,
    Twinkling the audacious leaves between,
Till round they turn and down they nestle—
    Is not the dear mark still to be seen?

Where I find her not, beauties vanish;
    Whither I follow her, beauties flee;
Is there no method to tell her in Spanish
    June's twice June since she breathed it with me?
Come, bud, show me the least of her traces,
    Treasure my lady's lightest footfall!
—Ah, you may flout and turn up your faces—
    Roses, you are not so fair after all!

JONES VERY   1813—80

The Garden

I saw the spot where our first parents dwelt;
And yet it wore to me no face of change.
And while amid its fields and groves, I felt
As if I had not sinned, nor thought it strange;
My eye seemed but a part of every sight,
My ear heard music in each sound that rose;
Each sense forever found a new delight,
Such as the spirit's visions only knows;
Each act some new and ever-varying joy
Did by my Father's love for me prepare;
To dress the spot my ever fresh employ,
And in the glorious whole with Him to share;
No more without the flaming gate to stray,
No more for sin's dark stain the debt of death to pay.

This Compost

I

Something startles me where I thought I was safest,
I withdraw from the still woods I loved,
I will not go now on the pastures to walk,
I will not strip the clothes from my body to meet
                                    my loveer the sea,
I will not touch my flesh to the earth as to other flesh
                                    to renew me.

O how can it be that the ground itself does not sicken?
How can you be alive you growths of spring?
How can you furnish health you blood of herbs,
                                    roots, orchards, grain?
Are they not continually putting distemper'd
                                    corpses within you?
Is not every continent work'd over and over
                                    with sour dead?

Where have you disposed of their carcasses?
Those drunkards and gluttons of so many generations?
Where have you drawn off all the foul liquid and meat?
I do not see any of it upon you to-day, or perhaps
                                    I am deceiv'd,
I will run a furrow with my plough, I will press my
          spade through the sod and turn it up underneath,
I am sure I shall expose some of the foul meat.

II

Behold this compost! behold it well!
Perhaps every mite has once form'd part of a sick
                                    person—yet behold!
The grass of spring covers the prairies,
The bean bursts noiselessly through the mould
                                    in the garden,
The delicate spear of the onion pierces upward,
The apple-buds cluster together on the apple-branches,
The resurrection of the wheat appears with pale visage
                                    out of its graves,
The tinge awakes over the willow-tree and the
                                    mulberry-tree,
The he-birds carol mornings and evenings while the
                                    she-birds sit on their nests,

The young of poultry break through the hatch'd eggs,
The new-born of animals appear, the calf is dropt from
                          the cow, the colt from the mare,
Out of its little hill faithfully rise the potato's dark
                                              green leaves,
Out of its hill rises the yellow maize-stalk, the lilacs
                              bloom in the dooryards,
The summer growth is innocent and disdainful above
                        all those strata of sour dead.
What chemistry!
That the winds are really not infectious,
That this is no cheat, this transparent green-wash of
                    the sea which is so amorous after me,
That it is safe to allow it to lick my naked body all over
                                          with its tongues,
That it will not endanger me with the fevers that have
                          deposited themselves in it,
That all is clean forever and forever,
That the cool drink from the well tastes so good,
That blackberries are so flavorous and juicy,
That the fruits of the apple-orchard and the
      orange-orchard, that melons, grapes, peaches, plums,
                          will none of them poison me,
That when I recline on the grass I do not catch
                              any disease,
Though probably every spear of grass rises out of what
                        was once a catching disease.

Now I am terrified at the Earth, it is that calm
                              and patient,
It grows such sweet things out of such corruptions,
It turns harmless and stainless on its axis, with such
                    endless successions of diseas'd corpses,
It distills such exquisite winds out of such
                                      infused fetor,
It renews with such unwitting looks its prodigal,
                          annual, sumptuous crops,
It gives such divine materials to men, and accepts such
                          leavings from them at last.

The Arbour

I'll rest me in this sheltered bower,
And look upon the clear blue sky
That smiles upon me through the trees,
Which stand so thickly clustering by;

And view their green and glossy leaves,
All glistening in the sunshine fair;
And list the rustling of their boughs,
So softly whispering through the air.

And while my ear drinks in the sound,
My wingèd soul shall fly away;
Reviewing long departed years
As one mild, beaming, autumn day;

And soaring on to future scenes,
Like hills and woods, and valleys green,
All basking in the summer's sun,
But distant still, and dimly seen.

Oh, list! 'tis summer's very breath
That gently shakes the rustling trees—
But look! the snow is on the ground—
How can I think of scenes like these?

'Tis but the *frost* that clears the air,
And gives the sky that lovely blue;
They're smiling in a *winter's* sun,
Those evergreens of sombre hue.

And winter's chill is on my heart—
How can I dream of future bliss?
How can my spirit soar away,
Confined by such a chain as this?

Under the Locust Blossoms

Under the locust blossoms
That hung and smelt like grapes :
Under the honey-locust blossoms,—
Faintly their breath escapes
And smites my heart; though years have passed since I
Beheld those clusters swinging silently,
Silver racemes against that sunset sky :

A sky all over rosy.
I waited for the night
Till the crickets tinkled drowsy
In their beds of clover white
Or fell silent at my footfall, one by one.
Did I wait ? Did I wander there alone,
Under shadow, in that garden not my own ?

'Tis but a shade of odour,
A recollected breath,
And I stand, a dark intruder
The swaying flowers beneath,
Alone, and peering on through anxious gloom
For a motion, for a glimmer; did it come ?
Oh that moment ! Oh that breath of locust bloom !

Lines Written in Kensington Gardens

In this lone, open glade I lie,
Screened by deep boughs on either hand;
And at its end, to stay the eye,
Those black-crowned, red-boled pine-trees stand!

Birds here make song, each bird has his,
Across the girdling city's hum.
How green under the boughs it is!
How thick the tremulous sheep-cries come!

Sometimes a child will cross the glade
To take his nurse his broken toy;
Sometimes a thrush flit overhead
Deep in her unknown day's employ.

Here at my feet what wonders pass,
What endless, active life is here!
What blowing daisies, fragran grass!
An air-stirred forest, fresh and clear.

Scarce fresher is the mountain-sod
Where the tired angler lies, stretched out,
And, eased of basket and of rod,
Counts his day's spoil, the spotted trout.

In the huge world, which roars hard by,
Be others happy if they can!
But in my helpless cradle I
Was breathed on by the rural Pan.

I, on men's impious uproar hurled,
Think often, as I hear them rave,
That peace has left the upper world
And now keeps only in the grave.

Yet here is peace for ever new!
When I who watch them am away,
Still all things in this glade go through
The changes of their quiet day.

Then to their happy rest they pass !
The flowers upclose, the birds are fed.
The night comes down upon the grass,
The child sleeps warmly in his bed.

Calm soul of all things ! make it mine
To feel, amid the city's jar,
That there abides a peace of thine,
Man did not make, and cannot mar.

FRANCIS TURNER PALGRAVE   1824—97

Eutopia

There is a garden where lilies
    And roses are side by side ;
And all day between them in silence
    The silken butterflies glide.

I may not enter the garden,
    Though I know the road thereto ;
And morn by morn to the gateway
    I see the children go.

They bring back light on their faces ;
    But they cannot bring back to me
What the lilies say to the roses,
    Or the songs of the butterflies be.

Along the garden terrace
FROM 'MODERN LOVE'

Along the garden terrace, under which
A purple valley (lighted at its edge
By smoky torch-flame on the long cloud-ledge
Whereunder dropped the chariot), glimmers rich,
A quiet company we pace, and wait
The dinner-bell in prae-digestive calm.
So sweet up violet banks the Southern balm
Breathes round, we care not if the bell be late:
Though here and there grey seniors question Time
In irritable coughings. With slow foot
The low rosed moon, the face of Music mute,
Begins among her silent bars to climb.
As in and out, in silvery dusk, we thread,
I hear the laugh of Madam, and discern
My Lady's heel before me at each turn.
Our tragedy, is it alive or dead?

DANTE GABRIEL ROSSETTI   1828–82

The Trees of the Garden

Ye who have passed Death's haggard hills; and ye
    Whom trees that knew your sires shall cease to know
    And still stand silent:—is it all a show—
A wisp that laughs upon the wall?—decree
Of some inexorable supremacy
    Which ever, as man strains his blind surmise
    From depth to ominous depth, looks past his eyes,

Sphinx-faced with unabashèd augury?
Nay, rather question the Earth's self. Invoke
    The storm-felled forest-trees moss-grown to-day
    Whose roots are hillocks where the children play;
Or ask the silver sapling 'neath what yoke
Those stars, his spray-crown's clustering gems,
                                        shall wage
Their journey still when his boughs shrink with age.

I haven't told my garden yet—

I haven't told my garden yet—
Lest that should conquer me.
I haven't quite the strength now
To break it to the Bee—

I will not name it in the street
For shops would stare at me—
That one so shy—so ignorant
Should have the face to die.

The hillsides must not know it—
Where I have rambled so—
Nor tell the loving forests
The day that I shall go—

Nor lisp it at the table—
Nor heedless by the way
Hint that within the Riddle
One will walk today—

We should not mind so small a flower—

We should not mind so small a flower—
Except it quiet bring
Our little garden that we lost
Back to the Lawn again.

So spicy her Carnations nod—
So drunken, reel her Bees—
So silver steal a hundred flutes
From out a hundred trees—

That whoso sees this little flower
By faith may clear behold
The Bobolinks around the throne
And Dandelions gold.

My Garden

A garden is a lovesome thing, God wot!
  Rose plot,
  Fringed pool,
Fern'd grot—
  The veriest school
  Of peace; and yet the fool
Contends that God is not—
Not God! in gardens! when the eve is cool?
  Nay, but I have a sign;
  'Tis very sure God walks in mine.

Once for All (Margaret)

I said: This is a beautiful fresh rose.
  I said: I will delight me with its scent,
  Will watch its lovely curve of languishment,
Will watch its leaves unclose, its heart unclose.
I said: Old earth has put away her snows,
  All living things make merry to their bent,
  A flower is come for every flower that went
In autumn, the sun glows, the south wind blows.
So walking in a garden of delight
  I came upon one sheltered shadowed nook
Where broad leaf shadows veiled the day with night
  And there lay snow unmelted by the sun:—
I answered: Take who will the path I took,
  Winter nips once for all: love is but one.

Thunder in the Garden

When the boughs of the garden hang heavy with rain
And the blackbird reneweth his song,
And the thunder departing yet rolleth again,
I remember the ending of wrong.

When the day that was dusk while his death was aloof
Is ending wide-gleaming and strange
For the clearness of all things beneath the world's roof,
I call back the wild chance and the change.

For once we twain sat through the hot afternoon
While the rain held aloof for a while,
Till she, the soft-clad, for the glory of June
Changed all with the change of her smile.

For her smile was of longing, no longer of glee,
And her fingers, entwined with mine own,
With caresses unquiet sought kindness of me
For the gift that I never had known.

Then down rushed the rain, and the voice
                                    of the thunder
Smote dumb all the sound of the street,
And I to myself was grown nought but a wonder,
As she leaned down my kisses to meet.

That she craved for my lips that had craved
                                    her so often,
And the hand that had trembled to touch,
That the tears filled her eyes I had hoped not to soften
In this world was a marvel too much.

It was dusk 'mid the thunder, dusk e'en as the night,
When first brake out our love like the storm,
But no night-hour was it, and back came the light
While our hands with each other were warm.

And her smile killed with kisses, came back as at first
As she rose up and led me along,
And out to the garden, where nought was athirst,
And the blackbird renewing his song.

Earth's fragrance went with her, as in the wet grass,
Her feet little hidden were set;
She bent down her head, 'neath the roses to pass,
And her arm with the lily was wet.

In the garden we wandered while day waned apace
And the thunder was dying aloof;
Till the moon o'er the minster-wall lifted his face,
And grey gleamed out the lead of the roof.

Then we turned from the blossoms, and cold
                                    were they grown:
In the trees the wind westering moved;
Till over the threshold back fluttered her gown,
And in the dark house was I loved.

ALGERNON CHARLES SWINBURNE   1837–1909

A Forsaken Garden
ISLE OF WIGHT

In a coign of the cliff between lowland and highland,
    At the sea-down's edge between windward and lee.
Walled round with rocks as an inland island,
    The ghost of a garden fronts the sea.
A girdle of brushwood and thorn encloses
    The steep square slope of the blossomless bed
Where the weeds that grew green from the graves
                                    of its roses
    Now lie dead.

The fields fall southward, abrupt and broken,
    To the low last edge of the long lone land.
If a step should sound or a word be spoken,
    Would a ghost not rise at the strange guest's hand?
So long have the grey bare walks lain guestless,
    Through branches and briars if a man make way,
He shall find no life but the sea-wind's, restless
    Night and day.

The dense hard passage is blind and stifled
    That crawls by a track none turn to climb
To the strait waste place that the years have rifled
    Of all but the thorns that are touched not of time.
The thorns he spares when the rose is taken;
    The rocks are left when he wastes the plain.
The wind that wanders, the weeds wind-shaken.
        These remain.

Not a flower to be pressed of the foot that falls not;
    As the heart of a dead man the seed-plots are dry;
From the thicket of thorns whence the nightingale
                                        calls not.
    Could she call, there were never a rose to reply.
Over the meadows that blossom and wither
    Rings but the note of a sea-bird's song:
Only the sun and the rain come hither
        All year long.

The sun burns sere and the rain dishevels
    One gaunt bleak blossom of scentless breath.
Only the wind here hovers and revels
    In a round where life seems barren as death.
Here there was laughing of old, there was weeping,
    Haply, of lovers none ever will know,
Whose eyes went seaward a hundred sleeping
        Years ago.

Heart handfast in heart as they stood, 'Look thither,'
    Did he whisper? 'look forth from the flowers
                                        to the sea:
For the foam-flowers endure when the
                                rose-blossoms wither.
    And men that love lightly may die—but we?'
And the same wind sang and the same waves whitened,
    And or ever the garden's last petals were shed,
In the lips that had whispered, the eyes
                                that had lightened,
        Love was dead.

Or they loved their life through, and then
                                        went whither?
And were one to the end—but what end who knows?
Love deep as the sea as a rose must wither,
    As the rose-red seaweed that mocks the rose.
Shall the dead take thought for the dead to love them?
    What love was ever as deep as a grave?
They are loveless now as the grass above them
    Or the wave.

All are at one now, roses and lovers,
    Not known of the cliffs and the fields and the sea.
Not a breath of the time that has been hovers
    In the air now soft with a summer to be.
Not a breath shall there sweeten the seasons hereafter
    Of the flowers or the lovers that laugh now or weep,
When as they that are free now of weeping and laughter
    We shall sleep.

Here death may deal not again for ever;
    Here change may come not till all change end.
From the graves they have made they shall
                                        rise up never,
    Who have left nought living to ravage and rend.
Earth, stones, and thorns of the wild ground growing,
    While the sun and the rain live, these shall be;
Till a last wind's breath upon all these blowing
    Roll the sea.

Till the slow sea rise and the sheer cliff crumble,
    Till terrace and meadow the deep gulfs drink,
Till the strength of the waves of the high tides humble
    The fields that lessen, the rocks that shrink,
Here now in his triumph where all things falter,
    Stretched out on the spoils that his own hand spread,
As a god self-slain on his own strange altar,
    Death lies dead.

A Garden Song

Here, in this sequestered close
Bloom the hyacinth and rose;
Here beside the modest stock
Flaunts the flaring hollyhock;
Here, as everywhere, one sees
Ranks, condition, and degrees.

All the seasons run their race
In this quiet resting place;
Peach, and apricot, and fig
Here will ripen, and grow big;
Here is store and overplus,—
More had not Alcinous!

Here, in alleys cool and green,
Far ahead the thrush is seen;
Here along the southern wall
Keeps the bee his festival;
All is quiet else—afar
Sounds of toil and turmoil are.

Here be shadows large and long;
Here be spaces meet for song;
Grant, O garden-god, that I,
Now that mood and moment please,
Find the fair Pierides!

A Spellbound Palace
HAMPTON COURT

On this kindly yellow day of mild low-travelling
                                        winter sun
        The stirless depths of the yews
        Are vague with misty blues :
Across the spacious pathways stretching spires of
                                        shadow run,
And the wind-gnawed walls of ancient brick are
                                        fired vermilion.

Two or three early sanguine finches tune
Some tentative strains, to be enlarged by May or June :
        From a thrush or blackbird
        Comes now and then a word,
While an enfeebled fountain somewhere within
                                        is heard.

        Our footsteps wait awhile,
        Then draw beneath the pile,
        When an inner court outspreads
        As 'twere History's own aisle,
Where the now-visioned fountain its attenuate
                                        crystal sheds
In passive lapse that seems to ignore the yon world's
                                        clamorous clutch,
And lays an insistent numbness on the place, like a
                                        cold hand's touch.

And there swaggers the Shade of a straddling King,
                        plumed, sworded, with sensual face,
And lo, too, that of his Minister, at a bold
                                        self-centred pace :
Sheer in the sun they pass ; and thereupon all is still,
Save the mindless fountain tinkling on with thin
                                        enfeebled will.

The Lodging-house Fuchsias

Mrs Masters's fuchsias hung
Higher and broader, and brightly swung,
   Bell-like, more and more
Over the narrow garden-path,
Giving the passer a sprinkle-bath
     In the morning.

She put up with their pushful ways,
And made us tenderly lift their sprays,
   Going to her door:
But when her funeral had to pass
They cut back all the flowery mass
     In the morning.

Song

I made another garden, yea,
　For my new Love:
I left the dead rose where it lay
　And set the new above.
Why did my Summer not begin?
　Why did my heart not haste?
My old Love came and walk'd therein,
　And laid the garden waste.

She enter'd with her weary smile,
　Just as of old;
She look'd around a little while
　And shiver'd with the cold:
Her passing touch was death to all,
　Her passing look a blight;
She made the white rose-petals fall,
　And turn'd the red rose white.

Her pale robe clinging to the grass
　Seem'd like a snake
That bit the grass and ground, alas!
　And a sad trail did make.
She went up slowly to the gate,
　And then, just as of yore,
She turn'd back at the last to wait
　And say farewell once more.

Cheddar Pinks

Mid the squander'd colour
  idling as I lay
Reading the Odyssey
  in my rock-garden
I espied the cluster'd
  tufts of Cheddar pinks
Burgeoning with promise
  of their scented bloom
All the modish motley
  of their bloom to-be
Thrust up in narrow buds
  on the slender stalks
Thronging springing urgent
  hasting (so I thought)
As if they fear'd to be
  too late for summer—
Like schoolgirls overslept
  waken'd by the bell
Leaping from bed to don
  their muslin dresses
    On a May morning:

Then felt I like to one
  indulging in sin
(Whereto Nature is oft
  a blind accomplice)
Because my aged bones
  so enjoy'd the sun
There as I lay alone
  idling with my thoughts
Reading an old poet
  while the busy world
Toil'd moil'd fuss'd and scurried
  worried bought and sold
Plotted stole and quarrel'd
  fought and God knows what.
I had forgotten Homer
  dallying with my thoughts
Till I fell to making
  these little verses
Communing with the flowers
  in my rock-garden
    On a May morning.

The Garden in September

Now thin mists temper the slow-ripening beams
Of the September sun: his golden gleams
On gaudy flowers shine, that prank the rows
Of high-grown hollyhocks, and all tall shows
That Autumn flaunteth in his bushy bowers;
Where tomtits, hanging from the drooping heads
Of giant sunflowers, peck the nutty seeds;
And in the feathery aster bees on wing
Seize and set free the honied flowers,
Till thousand stars leap with their visiting:
While ever across the path mazily flit,
Unpiloted in the sun,
The dreamy butterflies
With dazzling colours powdered and soft glooms,
White, black and crimson stripes, and peacock eyes,
Or on chance flowers sit,
With idle effort plundering one by one
The nectaries of deepest-throated blooms.

    With gentle flaws the western breeze
Into the garden saileth,
Scarce here and there stirring the single trees,
For his sharpness he vaileth:
So long a comrade of the bearded corn,
Now from the stubbles whence the shocks are borne,
O'er dewy lawns he turns to stray,
As mindful of the kisses and soft play
Wherewith he enamoured the light-hearted May,
Ere he deserted her;
Lover of fragrance, and too late repents;
Nor more of heavy hyacinth now may drink,
Nor spicy pink,
Nor summer's rose, nor garnered lavender,
But the few lingering scents
Of streakèd pea, and gillyflower, and stocks
Of courtly purple, and aromatic phlox.

And at all times to hear are drowsy tones
Of dizzy flies, and humming drones,
With sudden flap of pigeon wings in the sky,
Or the wild cry
Of thirsty rooks, that scour ascare
The distant blue, to watering as they fare
With creaking pinions, or—on business bent,
If aught their ancient polity displease,—
Come gathering to their colony, and there
Settling in ragged parliament,
Some stormy council hold in the high trees.

A Garden Song

I scorn the doubts and cares that hurt
   The world and all its mockeries,
My only care is now to squirt
   The ferns among my rockeries.

In early youth and later life
   I've seen an up and seen a down,
And now I have a loving wife
   To help me peg verbena down.

Of joys that come to womankind
   The loom of fate doth weave her few,
But here are summer joys entwined
   And bound with golden feverfew,

I've learnt the lessons one and all
   With which the world its sermon stocks,
Now, heedless of a rise or fall,
   I've Brompton and I've German stocks.

In peace and quiet pass our days,
   With nought to vex our craniums,
Our middle beds are all ablaze
   With red and white geraniums.

And like a boy I laugh when she,
   In Varden hat and Varden hose,
Comes slyly up the lawn at me
   To squirt me with the garden hose.

Let him who'd have the peace he needs
   Give all his worldly mumming up,
Then dig a garden, plant the seeds,
   And watch the product coming up.

To a Gardener

Friend, in my mountain-side demesne,
My plain-beholding, rosy, green
And linnet-haunted garden-ground,
Let still the esculents abound.
Let first the onion flourish there,
Rose among roots, the maiden-fair,
Wine-scented and poetic soul
Of the capacious salad bowl.
Let thyme the mountaineer (to dress
The tinier birds) and wading cress,
The lover of the shallow brook,
From all my plots and borders look.
Nor crisp and ruddy radish, nor
Pease-cods for the child's pinafore
Be lacking; nor of salad clan
The last and least that ever ran
About great nature's garden-beds.
Nor thence be missed the speary heads
Of artichoke; nor thence the bean
That gathered innocent and green
Outsavours the belauded pea.

These tend, I prithee; and for me,
Thy most long-suffering master, bring
In April, when the linnets sing
And the days lengthen more and more
At sundown to the garden door.
And I, being provided thus,
Shall, with superb asparagus,
A book, a taper, and a cup
Of country wine, divinely sup.

Magdalen Walks

The little white clouds are racing over the sky,
  And the fields are strewn with the gold of the
                          flower of March,
  The daffodil breaks under foot, and the tasselled larch
Sways and swings as the thrush goes hurrying by.

A delicate odour is borne on the wings of the
                          morning breeze,
  The odour of deep wet grass, and of brown
                          new-furrowed earth,
  The birds are singing for joy of the Spring's glad birth,
Hopping from branch to branch on the rocking trees.

And all the woods are alive with the murmur and
                          sound of spring,
  And the rose-bud breaks into pink on the
                          climbing briar,
  And the crocus-bed is a quivering moon of fire
Girdled round with the belt of an amethyst ring.

And the plane to the pine-tree is whispering some
                          tale of love
  Till it rustles with laughter and tosses its
                          mantle of green,
  And the gloom of the wych-elm's hollow is lit with
                          the iris sheen
Of the burnished rainbow throat and the silver breast
                          of a dove.

See! the lark starts up from his bed in the
                          meadow there,
  Breaking the gossamer threads and the nets of dew,
  And flashing adown the river, a flame of blue!
The kingfisher flies like an arrow, and wounds the air.

And the sense of my life is sweet! though I know that
                          the end is nigh:
  For the ruin and rain of winter will shortly come,
  The lily will lose its gold, and the chestnut-bloom
In billows of red and white on the grass will lie.

And even the light of the sun will fade at the last,
And the leaves will fall, and the birds will
                                   hasten away,
And I will be left in the snow of a flowerless day
To think on the glories of Spring, and the joys of a
                                   youth long past.

Yet be silent, my heart! do not count it a
                                   profitless thing
To have seen the splendour of the sun, and of grass,
                                   and of flower!
To have lived and loved! for I hold that to love
                                   for an hour
Is better for man and for woman than cycles of
                                   blossoming Spring.

A Garden Enclosed

Deep in this garden, closely fenced
  And wardered by a myriad eyes,
A world from time and space condensed,
  Feast for the weary idler lies.

Here at his earth-works plain to see
  Laborious toils the Roman ant;
Greek-like the honey-laden bee
  Mellifluous hangs from plant to plant.

The wary spider sports his thread
  And devil-like receives his toll;
And underground with buried head
  Grubs old mortality the mole.

Here wisdom waits the idler's look:
  The mind is free to roam or halt;
The garden is my history book,
  Its walls are my ancestral vault:

A book with fair devices strawed,
  Lavish in rosemary and sage;
Where all the margin-paths run broad
  Around the decorative page.

Or, open to the skies, a vault
  Where basking sunnily I lie,
And, negligent to Time's assault,
  With foot in earth prepare to die.

The Beloved

Blow gently over my garden,
Wind of the Southern sea,
In the hour that my Love cometh
    And calleth me!
My Love shall entreat me sweetly,
    With voice like the wood-pigeon;
'I am here at the gate of thy garden,
    Here in the dawn.'

Then I shall rise up swiftly
    All in the rose and grey,
And open the gate to my Lover
    At dawning of day.
He hath crowns of pain on His forehead,
    And wounds in His hands and feet;
But here mid the dews of my garden
    His rest shall be sweet.

Then blow not out of your forests,
    Wind of the icy North;
But Wind of the South that is healing
    Rise and come forth!
And shed your musk and your honey,
    And spill your odours of spice,
For one who forsook for my garden
    His Paradise!

Ancestral Houses
FROM 'MEDITATIONS IN TIME OF CIVIL WAR'

Surely among a rich man's flowering lawns,
Amid the rustle of his planted hills,
Life overflows without ambitious pains;
And rains down life until the basin spills,
And mounts more dizzy high the more it rains
As though to choose whatever shape it wills
And never stoop to a mechanical
Or servile shape, at others' beck and call.

Mere dreams, mere dreams! Yet Homer had not sung
Had he not found it certain beyond dreams
That out of life's own self-delight had sprung
The abounding glittering jet; though now it seems
As if some marvellous empty sea-shell flung
Out of the obscure dark of the rich streams,
And not a fountain, were the symbol which
Shadows the inherited glory of the rich.

Some violent bitter man, some powerful man
Called architect and artist in, that they,
Bitter and violent men, might rear in stone
The sweetness that all longed for night and day,
The gentleness none there had ever known;
But when the master's buried mice can play,
And maybe the great-grandson of that house,
For all its bronze and marble, 's but a mouse.

O what if gardens where the peacock strays
With delicate feet upon old terraces,
Or else all Juno from an urn displays
Before the indifferent garden deities;
O what if levelled lawns and gravelled ways
Where slippered Contemplation finds his ease
And childhood a delight for every sense,
But take our greatness with our violence?

What if the glory of escutcheoned doors,
And buildings that a haughtier age designed,
The pacing to and fro on polished floors
Amid great chambers and long galleries, lined
With famous portraits of our ancestors;
What if those things the greatest of mankind
Consider most to magnify, or to bless,
But take our greatness with our bitterness?

Sweet Dancer

The girl goes dancing there
On the leaf-sown, new-mown, smooth
Grass plot of the garden;
Escaped from bitter youth,
Escaped out of her crowd,
Or out of her black cloud.
Ah, dancer, ah, sweet dancer!

If strange men come from the house
To lead her away, do not say
That she is happy being crazy;
Lead them gently astray;
Let her finish her dance,
Let her finish her dance.
Ah, dancer, ah, sweet dancer!

The Glory of the Garden

Our England is a garden that is full of stately views,
Of borders, beds and shrubberies and lawns
　　　　　　　　　　　　　　and avenues,
With statues on the terraces and peacocks
　　　　　　　　　　　　　　strutting by;
But the Glory of the Garden lies in more than
　　　　　　　　　　　　　　meets the eye.

For where the old thick laurels grow, along the
　　　　　　　　　　　　　　thin red wall,
You find the tool- and potting-sheds which are the
　　　　　　　　　　　　　　heart of all;
The cold-frames and the hot-houses, the dungpits
　　　　　　　　　　　　　　and the tanks,
The rollers, carts and drain-pipes, with the barrows
　　　　　　　　　　　　　　and the planks.

And there you'll see the gardeners, the men
                                                and 'prentice boys
Told off to do as they are bid and do it without noise;
For, except when seeds are planted and we shout to
                                                scare the birds,
The Glory of the Garden it abideth not in words.

And some can pot begonias and some can bud a rose,
And some are hardly fit to trust with anything
                                                that grows;
But they can roll and trim the lawns and sift the sand
                                                and loam,
For the Glory of the Garden occupieth all who come.

Our England is a garden, and such gardens are not made
By singing:—'Oh, how beautiful!' and sitting
                                                in the shade,
While better men than we go out and start
                                                their working lives
At grubbing weeds from gravel-paths with broken
                                                dinner-knives.

There's not a pair of legs so thin, there's not a head
                                                so thick,
There's not a hand so weak and white, nor yet a heart
                                                so sick,
But it can find some needful job that's crying
                                                to be done,
For the Glory of the Garden glorifieth every one.

Then seek your job with thankfulness and work
                                                till further orders,
If it's only netting strawberries or killing slugs
                                                on borders;
And when your back stops aching and your hands
                                                begin to harden,
You will find yourself a partner in the Glory
                                                of the Garden.

Oh, Adam was a gardener, and God who made him sees
That half a proper gardener's work is done
                                                upon his knees,
So when your work is finished, you can wash your
                                                hands and pray
For the Glory of the Garden, that it may not pass away!
And the Glory of the Garden it shall never pass away!

Poem

TO ARTHUR EDMONDS

Geranium, houseleek, laid in oblong beds
On the trim grass. The daisies' leprous stain
Is fresh. Each night the daisies burst again,
Though every day the gardener crops their heads.

A wistful child, in foul unwholesome shreds,
Recalls some legend of a daisy chain
That makes a pretty necklace. She would fain
Make one, and wear it, if she had some threads.

Sun, leprous flowers, foul child. The asphalt burns,
The garrulous sparrows perch on metal Burns.
Sing! Sing! they say, and flutter with their wings.
He does not sing, he only wonders why
He is sitting there. The sparrows sing. And I
Yield to the strait allure of simple things.

The Garden of Shadow

Love heeds no more the sighing of the wind
Against the perfect flowers: thy garden's close
Is grown a wilderness, where none shall find
One strayed, last petal of one last year's rose.

O bright, bright hair! O mouth like a ripe fruit!
Can famine be so nigh to harvesting?
Love, that was songful, with a broken lute
In grass of graveyards goeth murmuring.

Let the wind blow against the perfect flowers,
And all thy garden change and glow with spring:
Love is grown blind with no more count of hours
Nor part in seed-time nor in harvesting.

The Malice-Dance

An intolerable singing
From an ancient haunted lawn
Where the ghost-moths whitely winging
Cross a moon-dial forlorn,
Drew me from you as you trifled
With the jasmin in your hair,
Dreaming that your beauty rifled
All my sense and held me there;
But I left you; and, escaping
With a lost tune in my head,
Set my memory reshaping
The old dances of the dead.
And the intolerable singing
Heard across that haunted lawn,
Drew me to the ghost-moths winging,
Round that moon-dial forlorn.
Over me the clouds were running
Races with the naked stars,
And dark Yews were making cunning
Love to whispering Deodars.
And the ghost-moths drugged my reason,
And I danced to that old tune
Malice dances full of treason
Round that dial of the moon!

Two Gardens

Two gardens see !—this, of enchanted flowers,
Strange to the eye, and more than earthly-sweet;
Small rivulets running, song-reëchoing bowers;
And green-walled pathways which, ere parting, meet;
And there a lion-like sun in heaven's delight
Breathes plenitude from dayspring to the night.

The other:—walls obscure, and chaces of trees,
Ilex and yew, and dream-enticing dark,
Hid pools, moths, creeping odours, silentness,
Luna its deity, and its watchward, *Hark!*
A still and starry mystery, wherein move
Phantoms of ageless wonder and of love.

Two gardens for two children—in one mind:
But ah, how seldom open now their gates I find!

The Deserted Garden

There is a garden in our square,
   And householders can have the key,
   On payment of an annual fee ;
   Yet no one enters there !

From August till the first of May,
   This garden is an empty place ;
   No puppy-dogs their tails may chase,
   No children romp and play !

Here faithful pug or Pekinese
   With chain and collar must be led,
   Lest he disturb some flower-bed
   That no one ever sees !

Here ragged urchins from the street
   Peer through the bars with wistful eyes
   On a deserted Paradise,
   Untrod by children's feet !

Some day, I know, with guilty grin,
   That garden gate I shall unlock,
   Collect this squalid little flock
   And lead them gaily in !

And, 'spite of by-laws and decrees,
   Poor Ponto's collar I'll detach,
   And let him run about and scratch,
   And scamper at his ease !

What matter then that neighbours glare
   At happy dog or grubby boys,
   If somebody at last enjoys
   The garden in our square ?

Time

'Established' is a good word, much used
                                        in garden books,
'The plant, when established' . . .
Oh, become established, quickly, quickly, garden!
For I am fugitive, I am very fugitive—

Those that come after me will gather these roses,
And watch, as I do now, the white wistaria
Burst, in the sunshine, from its pale green sheath.

Planned. Planted. Established. Then neglected,
Till at last the loiterer by the gate will wonder
At the old, old cottage, the old wooden cottage,
And say, 'One might build here, the view is glorious;
This must have been a pretty garden once.'

Putting in the Seed

You come to fetch me from my work to-night
When supper's on the table, and we'll see
If I can leave off burying the white
Soft petals fallen from the apple tree
(Soft petals, yes, but not so barren quite,
Mingled with these, smooth bean and wrinkled pea);
And go along with you ere you lose sight
Of what you came for and become like me,
Slave to a springtime passion for the earth.
How Love burns through the Putting in the Seed
On through the watching for that early birth
When, just as the soil tarnishes with weed,
The sturdy seedling with arched body comes
Shouldering its way and shedding the earth crumbs.

Song

If once I could gather in song
A flower from my garden of dreams—
    The dew from its petals unshaken,
    When starry and bright they awaken—
All men to the wonder would throng.

Though ever at dawning I go
By the marge of the life-giving streams
    That, shadow'd by blossoms upspringing,
    Remember the hills in their singing,
The fells of their birth in their flow;

Or early or late though I fare
To gather my garden of dreams
    For the barren, forsaken and lonely;
    I bring from the shadow-world only
Pale blossoms that perish in air.

The Innocent Spring
FROM 'THE SLEEPING BEAUTY'

In the great gardens, after bright spring rain,
We find sweet innocence come once again,
White periwinkles, little pensionnaires
With muslin gowns and shy and candid airs,

That under saint-blue skies, with gold stars sown,
Hide their sweet innocence by spring winds blown,
From zephyr libertines that like Richelieu
And d'Orsay their gold-spangled kisses blew;

And lilies of the valley whose buds blond and tight
Seem curls of little school-children that light
The priests' procession, when on some saint's day
Along the country paths they make their way;

Forget-me-nots, whose eyes of childish blue,
Gold-starred like heaven, speak of love still true;
And all the flowers that we call 'dear heart,'
Who say their prayers like children, then depart

Into the dark. Amid the dew's bright beams
The summer airs, like Weber waltzes, fall
Round the first rose who, flushed with her youth,
                                          seems
Like a young Princess dressed for her first ball:

Who knows what beauty ripens from dark mould
After the sad wind and the winter's cold?—
But a small wind sighed, colder than the rose
Blooming in desolation, 'No one knows.'

One Foot in Eden

One foot in Eden still, I stand
And look across the other land.
The world's great day is growing late,
Yet strange these fields that we have planted
So long with crops of love and hate.
Time's handiworks by time are haunted,
And nothing now can separate
The corn and tares compactly grown.
The armorial weed in stillness bound
About the stalk; these are our own.
Evil and good stand thick around
In the fields of charity and sin
Where we shall lead our harvest in.

Yet still from Eden springs the root
As clean as on the starting day.
Time takes the foliage and the fruit
And burns the archetypal leaf
To shapes of terror and of grief
Scattered along the winter way.
But famished field and blackened tree
Bear flowers in Eden never known.
Blossoms of grief and charity
Bloom in these darkened fields alone.
What had Eden ever to say
Of hope and faith and pity and love
Until was buried all its day
And memory found its treasure trove?
Strange blessings never in Paradise
Fall from these beclouded skies.

La Figlia che Piange

'O quam te memorem virgo . . .'

Stand on the highest pavement of the stair—
Lean on a garden urn—
Weave, weave the sunlight in your hair—
Clasp your flowers to you with a pained surprise—
Fling them to the ground and turn
With a fugitive resentment in your eyes:
But weave, weave the sunlight in your hair.

So I would have had him leave,
So I would have had her stand and grieve,
So he would have left
As the soul leaves the body torn and bruised,
As the mind deserts the body it has used.
I should find
Some way incomparably light and deft,
Some way we both should understand,
Simple and faithless as a smile and shake of the hand.

She turned away, but with the autumn weather
Compelled my imagination many days,
Many days and many hours:
Her hair over her arms and her arms full of flowers.
And I wonder how they should have been together!
I should have lost a gesture and a pose.
Sometimes these cogitations still amaze
The troubled midnight and the noon's repose.

The Garden

The ordered curly and plain cabbages
Are all set out like school-children in rows;
In six short weeks shall these no longer please,
For with that ink-proud lady the rose, pleasure goes.

I cannot think what moved the poet men
So to write panegyrics of that foolish
Simpleton—while wild rose as fresh again
Lives, and the drowsed cabbages keep soil coolish.

He spoke abrupt across my dream
FROM 'THE DEFEAT OF YOUTH'

He spoke abrupt across my dream: 'Dear Garden,
A stranger to your magic peace, I stand
Beyond your walls, lost in a fevered land
Of stones and fire. Would that the gods would harden
My soul against its torment, or would blind
Those yearning glimpses of a life at rest
In perfect beauty—glimpses at the best
Through unpassed bars. And here, without, the wind
Of scattering passion blows: and women pass
Glitter-eyed down putrid alleys where the glass
Of some grimed window suddenly parades—
Ah, sickening heart-beat of desire!—the grace
Of bare and milk-warm flesh: the vision fades,
And at the pane shows a blind tortured face.'

Gardener

Loveliest flowers, though crooked in their border,
And glorious fruit, dangling from ill-pruned boughs—
Be sure the gardener had not eye enough
To wheel a barrow between the broadest gates
Without a clumsy scraping.

Yet none could think it simple awkwardness;
And when he stammered of a garden-guardian,
Said the smooth lawns came by angelic favour,
The pinks and pears in spite of his own blunders,
They nudged at this conceit.

Well, he had something, though he called it nothing—
An ass's wit, a hairy-belly shrewdness
That would appraise the intentions of an angel
By the very yard-stick of his own confusion,
And bring the most to pass.

Home Thoughts in Laventie

Green gardens in Laventie!
Soldiers only know the street
Where the mud is churned and splashed about
By battle-wending feet;
And yet beside one stricken house there is a
                          glimpse of grass.
Look for it when you pass.

Beyond the church whose pitted spire
Seems balanced on a strand
Of swaying stone and tottering brick
Two roofless ruins stand,
And here behind the wreckage where the back wall
                          should have been
We found a garden green.

The grass was never trodden on,
    The little path of gravel
Was overgrown with celandine,
    No other folk did travel
Along its weedy surface, but the nimble-footed mouse
    Running from house to house.

So all among the vivid blades
    Of soft and tender grass
We lay, nor heard the limber wheels
    That pass and ever pass,
In noisy continuity until their very rattle
    Seems in itself a battle.

At length we rose up from this ease
    Of tranquil happy mind,
And searched the garden's little length
    A fresh pleasaunce to find;
And there some yellow daffodils and jasmine
                                            hanging high
    Did rest the tired eye.

The fairest and most fragrant
    Of the many sweets we found,
Was a little bush of daphne flower
    Upon a grassy mound,
And so thick were the blossoms set and so
                                        divine the scent
    That we were well content.

Hungry for spring, I bent my head,
    The perfume fanned my face,
And all my soul was dancing
    In that lovely little place,
Dancing with a measured step from wrecked and
                                        shattered towns
    Away upon the Downs.

I saw green banks of daffodil,
    Slim poplars in the breeze,
Great tan-brown hares in gusty March
    A-courting on the leas;
And meadows with their glittering streams, and silver
                                        scurrying dace,
    Home—what a perfect place!

Oh grateful colours, bright looks !

The grass is green
The tulip is red
A ginger cat walks over
The pink almond petals on the flower bed.
Enough has been said to show
It is life we are talking about. Oh
Grateful colours, bright looks! Well, to go
On. Fabricated things too—front doors and gates,
Bricks, slates, paving stones—are coloured
And as it has been raining and is sunny now
They shine. Only that puddle
Which, reflecting the height of the sky
Quite gives one a feeling of vertigo, shows
No colour, is a negative. Men!
Seize colours quick, heap them up while you can.
But perhaps it is a false tale that says
The landscape of the dead
Is colourless.

Jeremiah, the Tabby Cat, Stalks
in the Sunlit Garden

While you clamber over the blue gate in the garden,
In the sunlit garden I
Already arrived am before you: while
In a flash of the eye,
You are suspended in your leap
Against the blue ground of the gate. And then,
Unconscious cinema-actor, you cross your stage,
The plot where light cuts the shade like a jewel
On what intent?
Your eyes are amber in the sun, flashing
From the cushioned tuft of harebells
And calceolarias.
Now you thread the intricate pattern
Of garden stems and stems of shadow,
And cross the lawn:
Your supple flanks serpentine, your tread
Stealthy and secret, of who knows
What generations of jungle cats?
And so you reach the undergrowth of the sycamore;
Nor pause to hear me calling from my window
Whence sight of you I lose,
Your dappled side lost in the camouflage of shadow;
And you have left the sunlit garden
For who knows what memories of lost generations of
                                          great cats?

The Long Garden

It was the garden of the golden apples,
A long garden between a railway and a road,
In the sow's rooting where the hen scratches
We dipped our fingers in the pockets of God.

In the thistly hedge old boots were flying sandals
By which we travelled through the childhood skies,
Old buckets rusty-holed with half-hung handles
Were drums to play when old men married wives.

The pole that lifted the clothes-line in the middle
Was the flag-pole on a prince's palace when
We looked at it through fingers crossed to riddle
In evening sunlight miracles for men.

It was the garden of the golden apples,
And when the Carrick train went by we knew
That we could never die till something happened
Like wishing for a fruit that never grew,

Or wanting to be up on Candle-Fort
Above the village with its shops and mill.
The racing cyclists' gasp-gapped reports
Hinted of pubs where life can drink his fill.

And when the sun went down into Drumcatton
And the New Moon by its little finger swung
From the telegraph wires, we knew how God
                                        had happened
And what the blackbird in the whitethorn sang.

It was the garden of the golden apples,
The half-way house where we had stopped a day
Before we took the west road to Drumcatton
Where the sun was always setting on the play.

Snowfall on a College Garden

While we slept, these formal gardens
Worked into their disguise. The Warden's
Judas and tulip trees awake
In ermine. Here and there a flake
Of white falls from the painted scene,
Or a dark scowl of evergreen
Glares through the shroud, or a leaf dumps
Its load and the soft burden slumps
Earthward like a fainting girl.
No movement else. The blizzard's whirl
Froze to this cataleptic trance
Where nature sleeps and sleep commands
A transformation. See this bush
Furred and fluffed out like a thrush
Against the cold: snow which could snap
A robust veteran branch, piled up
On the razor edge of a weak spray,
Plumping it out in mimicry
Of white buddleia. Like the Elect
Ghosts of summer resurrect
In snowy robes. Only the twangling
Noise of unseen sparrows wrangling
Tells me that my window-view
Holds the garden I once knew.

The Progress of Poetry

I saw a Gardener with a watering can
Sprinkling dejectedly the heads of men
Buried up to their necks in the wet clay.

I saw a Bishop born in sober black
With a bewildered look on his small face
Being rocked in a cradle by a grey-haired woman.

I saw a man, with an air of painful duty
Binding his privates up with bunches of ribbon.
The woman who helped him was decently
                                        veiled in white.

I said to the Gardener: 'When I was a younger poet
At least my reference to death had some sonority.
I sang the danger and the deeps of love.

'Is the world poxy with a fresh disease?
Or is this a maggot I feel here, gnawing my breast
And wrinkling my five senses like a walnut's kernel?'

The Gardener answered: 'I am more vexed
                                        by the lichen
Upon my walls. I scraped it off with a space.
As I did so I heard a very human scream.

'In evening's sacred cool, among my bushes
A Figure was wont to walk. I deemed it angel.
But look at the footprint. There's hair
                                        between the toes!'

The Sunlight on the Garden

The sunlight on the garden
Hardens and grows cold,
We cannot cage the minute
Within its nets of gold,
When all is told
We cannot beg for pardon.

Our freedom as free lances
Advances towards its end;
The earth compels, upon it
Sonnets and birds descend;
And soon, my friend,
We shall have no time for dances.

The sky was good for flying
Defying the church bells
And every evil iron
Siren and what it tells:
The earth compels,
We are dying, Egypt, dying

And not expecting pardon,
Hardened in heart anew,
But glad to have sat under
Thunder and rain with you,
And grateful too
For sunlight on the garden.

Their Lonely Betters

As I listened from a beach-chair in the shade
To all the noises that my garden made,
It seemed to me only proper that words
Should be withheld from vegetables and birds.

A robin with no Christian name ran through
The Robin-Anthem which was all it knew.
And rustling flowers for some third party waited
To say which pairs, if any, should get mated.

Not one of them was capable of lying,
There was not one which knew that it was dying
Or could have with a rhythm or a rhyme
Assumed responsibility for time.

Let them leave language to their lonely betters
Who count some days and long for certain letters;
We, too, make noises when we laugh or weep:
Words are for those with promises to keep.

In Princes Street Gairdens

Doun by the baundstaund, by the ice-cream barrie,
there is a sait that says, Wilma is Fab.
Sit down aside me here and gieze your gab,   *give me your gossip*
jist you and me, a dou, and a wee cock-sparrie.   *pigeon*

Up in the street, shop-folk sairve and harrie;   *serve   plunder*
well-do-do weill-daean tredsmen scalte and pent and snab   *slate   paint   cobble*
carpenter and jyne and plaister. We never let dab   *say a word*
sae lang as we can jink the strait-and-narrie.   *dodge*

A sculptured growp, classical and symbolic,
Staunds by the path, maist beautiful to see:
National Savings, out for a bit frolic,   *a little*

peys echt per cent til Thrift and Industry,   *eight*
but dour Inflatioun, a diabolic
overcome dou, has owrecam, and duin Thrift in the ee.   *done   eye*

Scything

All day I swing my level scythe,
  Slow-marching on the severed swath;
Content to know myself alone
  With grass, and leaves, and gusty sun.

The random handle that I hold,
  A strong lopped bough, bone-dry, and curled,
Is emblem of an ancient time
  When wandering man first dreamed of home.

Scared by my near blade's foreign hiss
  A lizard flickers where I pass
Like Adam stooping to the ground
  With a lost Eden in his mind.

The Cold Green Element

At the end of the garden walk
the wind and its satellite wait for me;
their meaning I will not know
     until I go there,
but the black-hatted undertaker

who, passing, saw my heart beating in the grass,
is also going there. Hi, I tell him,
a great squall in the Pacific blew a dead poet
     out of the water,
who now hangs from the city's gates.

Crowds depart daily to see it, and return
with grimaces and incomprehension;
if its limbs twitched in the air
     they would sit at its feet
peeling their oranges.

And turning over I embrace like a lover
the trunk of a tree, one of those
for whom the lightning was too much
     and grew a brilliant
hunchback with a crown of leaves.

The ailments escaped from the labels
of medicine bottles are all fled to the wind;
I've seen myself lately in the eyes
     of old women,
spent streams mourning my manhood,

in whose old pupils the sun became
a bloodsmear on broad catalpa leaves
and hanging from ancient twigs,
     my murdered selves
sparked the air like the muted collisions

of fruit. A black dog howls down my blood,
a black dog with yellow eyes;
he too by someone's inadvertence
    saw the bloodsmear
on the broad catalpa leaves.

But the furies clear a path for me to the worm
who sang for an hour in the throat of a robin,
and misled by the cries of young boys
    I am again
a breathless swimmer in that cold green element.

LAWRENCE DURRELL   b.1912

In the Garden : Villa Cleobolus

The mixtures of this garden
Conduct at night the pine and oleander,
Perhaps married to dust's thin edge
Or lime where the cork-tree rubs
The quiet house, bruising the wall :

And dense the block of thrush's notes
Press like a bulb and keeping time
In this exposure to the leaves,
And as we wait the servant comes,
A candle shielded in the warm
Coarse coral of her hand, she weaves
A pathway for her in the golden leaves,
Gathers the books and ashtrays in her arm
Walking towards the lighted house,

Brings with her from the uninhabited
Frontiers of the darkness to the known
Table and tree and chair
Some half-remembered passage from a fugue
Played from some neighbour's garden
On an old horn-gramophone,

And you think: if given once
Authority over the word,
Then how to capture, praise or measure
The full round of this simple garden,
All its nonchalance at being,
How to adopt and raise its pleasure?

Press as on a palate this observed
And simple shape, like wine?
And from the many undeserved
Tastes of the mouth select the crude
Flavour of fruit in pottery
Coloured among this lovely neighbourhood?

Beyond, I mean, this treasure hunt
Of selves, the pains we sort to be
Confined within the loving chamber of a form,
Within a poem locked and launched
Along the hairline of the normal mind?

Perhaps not this: but somehow, yes,
To outflank the personal neurasthenia
That lies beyond in each expiring kiss:
Bring joy, as lustrous on this dish
The painted dancers motionless in play
Spin for eternity, describing for us all
The natural history of the human wish.

The Garden

It is a gesture against the wild,
The ungovernable sea of grass;
A place to remember love in,
To be lonely for a while;
To forget the voices of children
Calling from a locked room;
To substitute for the care
Of one querulous human
Hundreds of dumb needs.

It is the old kingdom of man.
Answering to their names,
Out of the soil the buds come,
The silent detonations
Of power wielded without sin.

Walking in Gardens

Walking in gardens by the sides
Of marble bathers toeing the garden ponds,
Skirting the ordered beds of paint-box flowers,
We spoke of drink and girls, for hours
Touched on the outskirts of the mind,
Then stirred a little chaos in the sun.
A new divinity, a god of wheels
Destroying souls and laying waste,
Trampling to dust the bits and pieces
Of faulty men and their diseases,
Rose in our outworn brains. We spoke our lines,
Made, for the bathers to admire,
Dramatic gestures in the air.
Ruin and revolution
Whirled in our words, then faded.
We might have tried light matches in the wind.
Over and round the ordered garden hummed,
There was no need of a new divinity,
No tidy flower moved, no bather gracefully
Lifted her marble foot, or lowered her hand
To brush upon the waters of the pond.

Winter Garden

The season's anguish, crashing whirlwind, ice,
Have passed, and cleansed the trodden paths
That silent gardeners have strewn with ash.

The iron circles of the sky
Are worn away by tempest;
Yet in this garden there is no more strife:
The Winter's knife is buried in the earth.
Pure music is the cry that tears
The birdless branches in the wind.
No blossom is reborn. The blue
Stare of the pond is blind.

And no-one sees
A restless stranger through the morning stray
Across the sodden lawn, whose eyes
Are tired of weeping, in whose breast
A savage sun consumes its hidden day.

Kensington Gardens

Old ladies and tulips, model boats,
Compact babies, mobile mothers,
Distant buses like parakeets,
Lonely men with mackintoshes
Over their arms—where do they go?
Where come from? now that summer's
Paraphernalia and splash is
Out, as if planted a year ago.

Unfriendly Flowers

Startled, the gardener learns to fear his art—
Seeing spring up, after long, loving hours
Of labour in the garden of his heart,
The vivid, the metallic the unfriendly flowers.

War

When the bloom is off the garden,
and I'm fighting in the sky,
when the lawns and flower beds harden,
and when weak birds starve and die,
and death-roll will grow longer,
eyes will be moist and red;
and the more I kill, the longer
shall I miss friends who are dead.

The Garden

The long curtained French-windows conceal
the company at dinner by candlelight.
I am the solitary person on the lawn,
dressed up silver by the moon.
The bush on my left sleeps, the tree on my right
is awake, but stays motionless to feel,

as I and Cupid on his ornament stone,
how the whole evening here discourses
and the stars too lean nearer to the earth,
for their traditional splendour pours forth
much more in such unpopulous places,
almost litters the trees like rain.

So the minutes assemble at first in silence
till here or there the speech of ghosts or leaves
is audible. And it appears each grieves,
the garden with its composite voice sighing:
*She does not come, and you who come instead
shew, by your attitude, she's dead.*

Daydream in a Sanctuary at Young Island, St Vincent

Walk in the enchanted garden
hahaha says the green bird
hahaha
the lady in the lilac silk
does not come here
the pale blue water
will spill
        and floating
yellow leaves will become boats
idle with no wind

(there is a fast white schooner
entering between the tall islands)

walk in the enchanted garden

prepare a dish of sand
and pebbles

float
within an idle yellow leaf

hahaha says the green
beaked bird
the lady in the lilac silk
does not walk here
        spill all the pale blue water.

O bright lady
in and upon
the dark silent water
walk
walk and bind
your lilac silk
over my burning eyes
walk and bind
your blinding black hair

in and upon
my empty hands

do not let the idle boats
windless
become drowned leaves
do not let the pale
(so delicately pale)
blue waters spill
and dry away
break the dish
of sand
and pebbles

scatter shells
scatter shells
scatter shells

hahaha says the green
beaked bird
hahaha

When will the fast
white schooner
sail between the tall islands
again?

O lady in
the lilac silk
walk in this enchanted garden
walk in this enchanted garden
walk here now.

LAURIS EDMOND   b.1924

Jardin des Colombières

It's the country of childhood
authentic fairyland—walled garden
silent under cypresses
wild violets, primroses awake
in a delicate wood, stone bridge
spanning the legendary stream
marble pillars, dim heraldic halls.

I am the child of exiles who dreamt
of the lost garden. Here it is earth
and boundaries—it is property;
the eyes at the shapely window
are sharp with calculation. You pay
six francs to enter; the other, more
melancholy, cost I do not know.

Garden, Wilderness

Green fingers, green hand, by now green man
All through, with sap for blood,
Menial to it, gross nature,
And governor of a green tribe
No law can tame, no equity can bend
From the sole need of each, to feed and seed,
Unless, refined beyond resistance to a blight
More grasping than their greed,
Rare shoots evade the keeper's pampering.

He goes to referee
A clinch of lupin, bindweed, common cleavers
And stinging nettle—each with a right to be
Where if one thrives the other three must weaken;
And with his green hand, kin to tendril, root,
Tugs at the wrestlers, to save, to separate
Although his green heart knows:
While sun and rain connive,
Such will the game remain, such his and their estate.

More rain than sunshine: his green lungs inhale
Air thick with horsetail spore,
Grass pollen; his legs trail
Trains of torn herbage, dragging through
                                    swollen growth
Twined, tangled with decay.
For his green food he gropes,
To taste his share, bonus of fruit and berry,
Tribute for regency,
Sweet compensation for defeated hopes
Or dole despite the drudgery, the waste.

A garden of the mind,
Pure order, equipoise and paradigm
His lord, long far away and silent, had designed,
With bodies, never his, indifferent machines
To impose it and maintain
Against the clinging strand, the clogging slime;
And best invisible, as now that lord's become
Whose ghost the green man serves; that
                                    contemplated flower
Whose day of stillness filled all space, all time.

Agony in any Garden

And anybody's agony might be
This garden and this time. A different prayer,
A hand put out with no one else to touch
And faltering stammered words that cannot bear
The breadth of passion—anyone might reach
His pitch of hopelessness. We judge despair

By who cries out, by greatness underneath.
The dark night and the friends who would not wake
Are where we choose to place them. Now and here
Dumbness between thumped ribs may tear and break
And some small whimper shelter a great fear.

Epitaph on a Fir-tree

She grew ninety years through sombre winter,
Rhododendron summer of midges and rain,
In a beechwood scarred by the auctioneer,

Till a March evening, the garden work done,
It seemed her long life had been completed,
No further growth, no gaiety could remain.

At a wedding breakfast bridesmaids planted
With trowel and gloves this imported fir.
How soon, measured by trees, the party ended.

Arbour and crinoline have gone under
The laurel, gazebos under the yews:
Wood for wood, we have little to compare.

We think no more of granite steps and pews,
Or an officer patched with a crude trepan
Who fought in Rangoon for these quiet acres.

Axes and saws now convert the evergreen
Imperial shadows into deal boards,
And let the sun enter our house again.

Quickly we'll spend the rings that she hoarded
In her gross girth. The evening is ours.
Those delicate girls who earthed her up are faded.

Except for daffodils, the ground is bare:
We two are left. They walked through pergolas
And planted well, so that we might do better.

The Garden of the Gods

All plants grow here ; the most minute,
   Glowing from turf, is in its place.
   The constant vision of the race :
Lawned orchard deep with flower and fruit.

So bright, that some who see it near
   Think there is lapis on the stems,
   And think green, blue, and crimson gems
Hang from the vines and briars here.

They follow path to path in wonder
   Through the intense undazzling light.
   Nowhere does blossom flare so white !
Nowhere so black is earthmold under !

It goes, though it may come again.
   But if at last they try to tell,
   They search for trope or parallel,
And cannot, after all, explain.

It was sufficient, there, to be,
   And meaning, thus, was superseded.
   —Night circles it, it has receded,
Distant and difficult to see.

Where my foot rests, I hear the creak
   From generations of my kin,
   Layer on layer, pressed leaf-thin.
They merely are. They cannot speak.

This was the garden's place of birth :
   I traced it downward from my mind,
   Through breast and calf I feel it vined
And rooted in the death-rich earth.

Her Garden

My grandmother grew tiny grapes and tiger-lilies,
But there is no sentimental cut to her garden
Through a fat album or remembered lane ;
Only interior voyages made on London ferries

Paddling the Thames' wicked brew to Silvertown,
Where regular as boot boys, the factories
Blacked her house every day, obscured the skies
And the town's sweet name at the railway station.

Between ships parked at the end of the road
And factory gates, she kept her home against soot,
Kept her garden colours in spite of it—
Five square feet of bitterness in a paved yard

Turned to the silent flowering of her will,
Loaded with dusty beauty and natural odours,
Cinnamon lilies, and the vine roots hanging grapes,
Sour as social justice, on the wash-house wall.

The Manor Garden

The fountains are dry and the roses over.
Incense of death. Your day approaches.
The pears fatten like little buddhas.
A blue mist is dragging the lake.

You move through the era of fishes,
The smug centuries of the pig—
Head, toe and finger
Come clear of the shadow. History

Nourishes these broken flutings,
These crowns of acanthus,
And the crow settles her garments.
You inherit white heather, a bee's wing,

Two suicides, the family wolves,
Hours of blankness. Some hard stars
Already yellow the heavens.
The spider on its own string

Crosses the lake. The worms
Quit their usual habitations.
The small birds converge, converge
With their gifts to a difficult borning.

Drawings

The ones not in the catalogue:
little sketches, done in her garden—this
head of a child (the same child
we saw in the picnic scene, remember?)
And trees, of course, and grasses,
and a study of hawthorn berries.
Doodles, unfinished drafts: look
at this chestnut leaf, abandoned in mid-
stroke—a telephone-call, perhaps;
a visitor; some interruption.

She may have been happier,
or happy longer, or at least more often . . .
but that's presumption. Let's move on:
grasses again; a group of stones
from her rockery, done in charcoal; and this
not quite completed pencil sketch of
a tiger lily, the springy crown
of petals curved back on itself
right to the stem, the long electric
stamens almost still vibrating.

Corners of a Circle

Flower seeds sown in trays
lined with papers reporting
calamities. How an anguished
face melts under the spray
from the fine rose. As if
to say, The trunk is brittle
as the tuber, deep down. As
if my chiseled minuteness
deep down in your crib . . .

I think of you as a cloud
thinks of a drop of water
released in multiplicity
and touching the earth, praised.

The Influence coming into Play:
The seven of pentacles

Under a sky the color of pea soup
she is looking at her work growing away there
actively, thickly like grapevines or pole beans
as things grow in the real world, slowly enough.
If you tend them properly, if you mulch, if you water,
if you provide birds that eat insects a home
                                    and winter food,
if the sun shines and you pick off caterpillars,
if the praying mantis comes and the ladybugs
                                    and the bees,
then the plants flourish, but at their own
                                    internal clock.

Connections are made slowly, sometimes they
                        grow underground.
You cannot tell always by looking what is happening.
More than half a tree is spread out in the soil
                        under your feet.
Penetrate quietly as the earthworm that blows
                        no trumpet.
Fight persistently as the creeper that brings
                        down the tree.
Spread like the squash plant that overruns the garden.
Gnaw in the dark and use the sun to make sugar.

Weave real connections, create real nodes, build
                        real houses.
Live a life you can endure: make love that is loving.
Keep tangling and interweaving and taking more in,
a thicket and bramble wilderness to the outside
                        but to us
interconnected with rabbit runs and burrows and lairs.

Live as if you liked yourself, and it may happen:
reach out, keep reaching out, keep bringing in.
This is how we are going to live for a long time:
                        not always,
for every gardener knows that after the digging, after
                        the planting.
after the long season of tending and growth, the
                        harvest comes.

The China Pear Trees

The power of three China pear trees
standing in their splintery timber bark
on an open paddock:

the selector's house that staked and watered them
in Bible times, beside a spaded patch
proved deciduous; it went away in loads,

but after sixty years of standing out,
vanishing in autumn, blizzarding in spring,
among the farmlands' sparse and giant furniture,

after sixty crops gorged on from all directions,
so that no windfalls, fermenting, shrank
                              to lizard-skinned
puree in the short grazed grass,

the trees drew another house, electrified and steaming
but tin-roofed as before for blazing clouds to creak over
and with tiny nude frogs upright again on lamplit glass;

they drew another kitchen garden, and a dam
half scintillating waterlily pleasance, half irrigation,
an ad hoc orchard, Christmas pines,
                              a cud-dropping mower;

they drew a wire fence around acres of enclosure
shaped like a fuel tin, its spout a tunnel of trees
tangled in passionflower and beige-belled wonga vine,

down inside which a floodtime waterfall churns
millet-sized gravel. And they called lush
                              water-leaved trees
like themselves to the stumpholes of gone rainforest

to shade with four seasons the tattered evergreen
oil-haloed face of a subtle fire landscape
(water forest versus fire forest, ancient war of the
   southern world).

It was this shade in the end, not their coarse
                                         bottling fruit
that mirrored the moist creek trees outward,
                                         as a culture
containing the old gardener now untying and
                                         heaping up

one more summer's stems and chutneys,
his granddaughter walking a horse the colour
                                         of her boots
and his tree-shaping son ripping out the odd
                                         failed seedling,
'Sorry, tree. I kill and I learn.'

Gardener

When they moved into the house it was winter.
In the garden a sycamore stood.
No other root nor shoot, but wild nettles
Good only for a bitter soup. He planned
Flowers around the sycamore for summer,
The great splayed rose, the military tulip,
All colours, smell of sun, himself with spade
Drinking cold beer with his wife. Spring came.
He rooted up the nettles with his hands.
He burnt them all, stamped on the clotted ash,
Tamping new seeds in, fingering stones aside.
This work he wanted, his hands came alive.
They wanted flowers to touch. But from his care
Only the tough nasturtiums came. They crawled
In sullen fire by the wall a week.
But the soil was sour, the roots went unfed.
Even they ceased to clutch, their heads fell forward.

All summer was the same. He fed the soil,
Flicking out stones, plucking the few sparse shoots.
The trapped flowers were trying to escape,
Bud died in their cells, and winter came.

Next year he planted early. Spring brought up
Over fussed tussocks, a green scanty surf.
Then it receded, but a tidewrack stayed
Of shrivelled leaves, shoots like dead dragonflies.
Then nettles crawled back. Now he didn't care.
His hands were useless, the earth was not his.
It did things to him, never he to it.
He watched the nettles with a little smile.

Then in the snowdrift of a summer bed
He planted himself, and a child came—
News that he knew early one winter day.
He came home dumbly from the hospital.
The garden gate was open. He went out,
Stood by the sycamore, watched the clouds moult,
Stood in the chilly and falling feathers
Under the sycamore, and not knowing why,
He felt his hands become alive, and touched
The tree's smooth body with a kind of joy,
Thinking next summer it would have new leaves.

Mr. McGregor's Garden

Some women save their sanity with needles.
I complicate my life with studies
Of my favourite rabbit's head, his vulgar volatility,
Or a little ladylike sketching
Of my resident toad in his flannel box;
Or search for handsome fungi for my tropical
Herbarium, growing dry-rot in the garden,
And wishing that the climate were kinder,
Turning over the spiky purple heads among the moss
With my cheese-knife to view the slimy veil.

Unlike the cupboard-love of sleepers in the siding,
My hedgehog's sleep is under his control
And not the weather's; he can rouse himself
At half-an-hour's notice in the frost, or leave at will
On a wet day in August, by the hearth.
He goes by breathing slowly, after a large meal,
A lively evening, very cross if interrupted,
And returns with a hundred respirations
To the minute, weak and nervous when he wakens,
Busy with his laundry.

On sleepless nights while learning
Shakespeare off by heart,
I feel that Bunny's at my bedside
In a white cotton nightcap,
Tickling me with his whiskers.